CW00520592

On Dusty Plains

CHARLES ADDISON

AUTHOR'S NOTE

During my time in Afghanistan, I made haphazard, mostly undated, hand-scribbled notes reporting what I had seen, thought, and felt. The account is based primarily on my notes, and my imperfect memory. My notes are mainly introspective in nature — they did not concern themselves with who was there with me, which vehicle I was in, which direction a patrol took, etc. In recreating my experiences, I have had to confabulate comrades to populate a patrol with me, or an IRT shout, or even a basic conversation over a cigarette. In my attempt to show the experience of Herrick 9 through the eyes of a Rifleman I have almost certainly attributed people present at events they were not. I have therefore redacted the real names of my comrades, to both protect their identities, and myself from the effects of any misremembering. Apologies to anyone who is ill-served by my recollections.

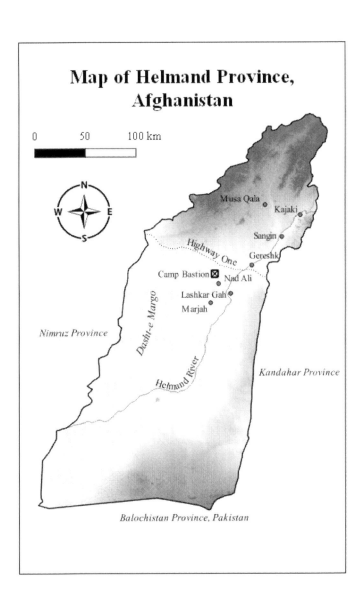

Map of Helmand Province, Afghanistan

0   50   100 km

N
W   E
S

Musa Qala
Kajaki
Sangin
Highway One
Gereshk
Camp Bastion ⊠ Nad Ali
Lashkar Gah
Marjah

Dasht-e Margo

Nimruz Province

Kandahar Province

Helmand River

Balochistan Province, Pakistan

CONTENTS

INTRODUCTION

To date, one hundred and six helicopters have been lost in Afghanistan during the ISAF era, either shot down by RPGs or heavy machinegun fire, or crashing in accidents, making it the most dangerous form of transport after foot. In the winter of 2008, British troops were locked in the bloodiest campaign since the Korean war over fifty years previously, and our helicopter fleet, precious and scarce, was stretched to its limit.

3 Commando Brigade were back after letting 16 Air Assault Brigade take the summer of fighting. Troops were holding platoon houses — barely protected mud-brick compounds in villages and towns — with six or eight men and a platoon of Afghans. Amidst this chaos I found myself barely out of basic training, trying to understand whether we were preventing the drugs trade, promoting women's rights and equality, maintaining border stability to protect a nuclear power nation, or prevent Afghanistan from being used to train terrorists.

Task Force Helmand had just been increased to ten thousand men, and although we held the centres of Musa Qala, Sangin, Kajaki, Gereshk and Lashkar Gah, outside the wire was a deadly no man's land. Minefields from the

Russian campaigns still littered the stony deserts, IEDs were growing ever more complex, and foreign fighters flooding in from Iran and Balochistan were learning how to survive against the British.

Support for the armed forces, to reach a post-Falklands high, would start to be eroded by the end of 2009 as boys and men from 2nd Battalion Rifle Regiment died trying to hold onto Sangin, before in the end we gave it away without a shot and abandoned the hard-won ground overnight. The evening news head and shoulders photo of a young soldier, perhaps two, sometimes three, staring out into the conscience of an immured population with old, old eyes set into his young face became a backdrop for the Fourth Afghan campaign. Against all this, my unit was tasked with providing infantrymen to the most dangerous helicopter mission in the world: The IRT. I was the third most junior Rifleman in my company, and this is the story of my life and my deployment to Afghanistan in the winter campaign of Operation Herrick 9.

PROLOGUE

I can run a mile and a half in eight minutes thirty, and fill a magazine with thirty rounds of NATO 5.56mm ammunition in less than one minute. I change my socks twice a day to keep trench foot at bay, and rise in the dark from a bivouac in a pine woodblock, silently pack my kit into fighting order and roll through dawn attacks with a platoon of men; firing countless rounds of ammunition in attack after attack through Brecon valleys and ranges. We are firing live rounds and throwing live grenades, to simulate the close-quarters fighting we are anticipating in Helmand province.

It is summer 2008, and my friends and I find ourselves training for war. We are attached to 1st Battalion Rifle Regiment, and my unit are from D Company in Plymouth, nicknamed The Bloody Eleventh. The Bloody Eleventh is a tight-knit group, and when the call came for Riflemen for an overseas deployment almost all the platoon volunteered. Now that we are here, the whole process is an endless administration nightmare, as we are bussed from barracks to barracks, Nottingham to Folkestone, Salisbury to Norfolk, staying at each camp for a few days. We stay to take a day or two of lessons on a particular bit of kit or fighting method, culminating in a final exercise that sees us sleep deprived, cold, wet, muddy, and thoroughly drilled in the modern methods of keeping the Russians at bay should they come at us through Germany. Every day of training we grow leaner and sharper, and every weekend of drunken debauchery finds us vomiting and stumbling through fitness training early on Monday morning.

The days advance, and our company is staged through fire and manoeuvre drills, and range days on weapon after weapon. We practise night shoots, march and shoots, shooting in the open, shooting from cover, shooting whilst we take ground, shooting whilst we retire, shooting from vehicles, until it feels like all the rounds in NATO have passed through the barrel of my LSW. I favour the LSW, heavier than a standard SA80 rifle and with a longer barrel, it also has a longer range, and I relish knocking down targets from six hundred metres away, dropping magazines to the floor and fitting new ones as fast as my well-drilled hands can manage.

We patrol out through a mock FOB on a blank fire exercise, somewhere in Norfolk. A FOB — forward operating base — is the modern low-tech fort, built like a child's castle of blocks from giant earth-filled steel mesh cubes called Hesco. The FOB is burlap clad, twenty feet high, with watch towers on each corner and soldiers encamped within. After only a lucky hour on sentry in the night, I am content and fresh, ready for whatever the morning will bring. I have been designated the boss's point man and runner, so I head the patrol with the boss behind me, steering me to his lead. The night's cold is in retreat, disarray, yet lingers stubbornly at the tips of my fingers as the morning sun noses over the trees ahead. We are moving cross country, across fields and brushland, our drab green combat jackets adorned with crisp fresh insignia — the skyward dagger of 3 Commando Brigade. The Rifle Regiment is providing infantrymen to the Commandos, and we are amongst them.

Today we are on combined exercise with Warrior armoured fighting vehicles, Apache gunships, Typhoon fast jet support, and notional artillery. I have my weapon set to fully automatic, to spray half a magazine of blanks in case of contact from a pretend enemy. Behind me the boss calls softly in his clipped, expensive accent for me to bear left slightly. The boss is around my age, but an officer in charge of a platoon of men, he is a breed apart — to be obeyed and feared, mocked and reviled and worshiped and followed, and all at once. The Danish officers, I will learn later, dine with their men, make small talk, learn about their loves and lives the better to lead them. The British still follow a rigid caste system where the officers and men are entirely, religiously, separate. I doubt the boss knows the first thing about me except my surname, possibly my Christian name and blood group if he is allowed to confer with the Platoon Serjeant, and that I am his runner and point man. And I don't know the first thing about him, truth be told. He is the boss, and that is all.

We are patrolling out to link up with the armoured Warrior vehicles, before we advance to take a position somewhere ahead. We are alone, a double column of infantry, our other platoons ranging wide on the flanks out of sight. I slow and take a knee, weapon in my shoulder as we come to the end of a shrub line, and the boss closes up behind me, guiding my next move, pointing out my next marker. I stand and move off, making a short, weaving dash as I cross an exposed stretch of open ground, my fighting gear heavy about my waist and weapon pumping side to side. At a hedgerow now, I take a knee again, take a breath, weapon up, and wait for the rest of the men behind me to close up.

The boss crosses too, and behind him comes Rifleman Peterson, an old salt of the Bloody Eleventh. Peterson is a disaster of a man as a civilian, having sold pyramid schemes, been fired from most jobs he held including pizza delivery boy, failed each year of university at least once. That he still maintains a permanent devil-may-care attitude is a source of amusement and awe. As a soldier, Peterson is tough as an old boot, fit as a fiddle, and ready for action.

Behind Peterson, Rifleman Smith cradles his weapon casually, stepping carefully and spitting with the wind. We joined at the same time, trained together, watched each other's backs throughout recruit training and deployment training. Smith is a man with a quick smile and warm laughter from his belly when the Bloody Eleventh stand together for the evening's beer.

Several men back is Lance Corporal Vince, a future officer but today one of the men. He is a consummate drunkard and a gentleman; always opinionated and eager to debate, always fair with his rank, he will be my section commander when we get to Afghanistan.

Eski is next, a veteran of previous Afghanistan deployments, younger than most of us but a source of information that we all defer to when he tells us what to expect of Afghanistan and the Taliban. Eski is fighting a losing battle with his appetite, and carries his frame slowly, suffering stoically as he does.

Next Chris, our Serjeant and the big brother of the platoon. Chris is the closest any of us come to responsible, as he has a house and a fiancé, a proper job, and as a veteran of the Iraq war, has done his share of soldiering to command the respect of the men who follow him. We will say goodbye when we get to Afghanistan, for he has been picked for attachment to a different unit, that will be operating out of Garmsir in the south of Helmand.

Chalky and Andy are out on the flank, they are the Cornish double-act, both former regular soldiers with the

Light Infantry, now aging infanteers with a wealth of experience from tours of duty in Northern Ireland and Kosovo. They are GPMG machine gunners, drivers, and eternal comedians who play off each other and can make the platoon's sides ache with laughter.

There are more of us, though unseen, off with Chalky's gun team or with Corporal Griff's reserve section. Litch, from Cornwall, his arms covered in tattoos, turns up his sleeves at every chance to show them off. Litch has left a pregnant girlfriend behind and run off on deployment with us, he worked fast, as he only had six months off since he was in Afghanistan last winter. Litch is the counterpoint to Chalky and Andy, as he is a constant complainer.

Flint is a student and army fanatic, splitting his time between poring over academic papers and volunteering for exercises with the regular army. His flat is piled high with military equipment, and he owns several rifles through a gun club.

Fisk is a grizzled veteran of the Iraq war, a Cornishman with a good shot and a bottomless thirst. Rumours abound of his first patrol in Iraq, where they stopped an Iraqi who pulled out a pistol. Fisk drew his quicker and killed with a single shot.

There are some from upcountry too, from C Company. Big Jimmy is a hulking man from Dorset, whose handshake breaks bones. Cooper is a wire-bodied skiver, a geezer, a mockney with countless ideas to make a quick buck that never come to anything.

Corporal Ozzy from New Zealand is part Maori, Ngabo a Kenyan, and Jacobs is a short and stocky chain-smoker.

Corporal Richards and Lance Corporal Bazza are from somewhere around Wiltshire, with country drawls and years of experience of soldiering. We do not have enough desert uniform to go around yet, so both of them wear green combat smocks when we arrive in Helmand.

Conlay and Bruce Lee are Bristolians, Bruce Lee a Kung-Fu fanatic and Conlay — well, Conlay is a strange one. But then we all are, in our way.

Ahead, small arms fire crackles and builds to a crescendo. I hit the ground, crawl to cover, and take a fire position, scanning the ground ahead. 1 Platoon have found an 'enemy' position: two Gurkhas in a copse, firing belts of blank ammunition from a GPMG. The boss moves his platoon to be held in reserve, whilst 1 Platoon bound up and fight through. We take position beside a tree block, waiting, whilst the crackles sound away to the north east. Eventually 1 Platoon clear the position, and we break out into patrol again. So our days are spent, patrol and fire and manoeuvre. That night back at the FOB, safe and warm, we eat cold rations and clean our weapons, fondly imagining that Afghanistan will be like this.

1. THE ROAD TO HELMAND

The rain is relentless, but it is so dark I can only see the downpour in the headlights of our convoy. We are stopped on the dirt track road to Highway One, a mile outside Camp Bastion, in the dead of night of an Afghanistan winter. I am standing beside my armoured vehicle, water dripping off my helmet and my sodden trousers plastered to my thighs. My machinegun is slung on my back and in my hands I hold a Vallon metal detector. Corporal Griff is briefing Litch and I on our task to clear the route for IEDs. I have only one chance to get it right, so Griff tells me.

Tonight's resupply convoy is headed to Musa Qala, and they have to take the same dirt track to Highway One every time they go north. This means the Taliban know the route they will use, and the IED risk is high. The IEDs the Taliban in our area use are pressure plates- improvised landmines rigged to explode when a foot steps on them, or a vehicle drives over them. They are simple, deadly, and commonplace in Helmand province. Though we have been here two months already, this is my first time using the metal detector — I have been lucky.

I pick up the metal detector and try to remember what I

was told during our IED briefing by the Royal Engineer IED search team, back in the English summertime before we arrived here. I turn the device on at the third attempt, and a baffling array of red lights is visible on a small panel. I brush my boot with the detector head and the red lights spike, detecting the metal eyelets. OK, red means metal. Simple enough. Griff walks me to the front of the convoy before I have time to think, and the wind cuts through me as we step beyond the shelter of the armoured vehicle, lashing rain stinging my face and hands.

Corporal Griff hurries back inside the armoured vehicle, and suddenly Litch and I are alone. I must cover a swathe of the dirt road for the left tyres of the convoy, sweeping the metal detector left and right as I proceed. Immediately as I set off, the red lights are spiking at every step. I walk forwards slowly, sweeping for metal, hoping that the metal detector will start working properly. With each step, every red flash seems the same as the last, which was bare road. Within a few steps my stomach drops, as I realise the metal detector is useless, and in the darkness I won't be able to see the tell-tale signs of IEDs — freshly turned earth, darker patches of ground or suspicious marks. I have the longest, hardest kilometres of my life to search for IEDs by proving the route safe with my feet.

Framed in the headlights of the lead vehicle and visible for miles around, Litch and I move forwards slowly, the convoy following at a respectful distance. I place each foot down warily, expecting the worst. We move on, inching our way closer to the junction with stuttering steps and mis-matched paces, sweeping and swaying, watching the red lights on the metal detector peak and spike like dancing fireflies. At 3 A.M. with my desert boots soaked through and my toes numb in heavy socks, I am loneliness incarnate. The rain wears on and my spirits wash around my feet. I pray.

Dear God, I'm sorry I don't believe in you. I promise I will start. God, please let the bomb be on his side of the road. I'm not ready to die. If I have to die out here, make it tomorrow. Please, give me one more day.

Deep down I know that it's a lie. I'm not going to keep my promise, and tomorrow I will still want one more day, then another, and another. I will never stop wanting one more day. The Vallon spikes red again, and I take another step forward. I sweep and walk onwards, nerves stretched, thinking no further than my next footfall.

2. LAST FLIGHT TO BASTION

Two months earlier, and we are flying to Afghanistan. Deep inside the transport plane, we are a mix of units from all of 3 Commando Brigade, all in fresh desert shirts, and all wearing a flak jacket and helmet. The hours weigh heavy, and unfamiliar faces around me gaze ahead blankly. I join them, my stomach heavy as stone and my head pounding.

My company had been sitting around on our kit at Brize Norton, the RAF transport hub that flies units to Afghanistan and Iraq for our six-month stints on operations. We are going to Operation Herrick, to Helmand, and to the Wild West frontier country of Afghanistan where civil laws are replaced by the Pashtunwali, a tribal code, and we will be the foreigners trying to tell friend from foe — and trusting none.

For days now my company has been flying small groups of men into Kandahar, and from there to Helmand and Camp Bastion. I find myself at the tail end of the procession. Lance Corporal Vince and I are the last from my platoon to make the flight, and we spent the last night in the bar at Brize Norton throwing down port and making merry until the small hours. Now, bleary eyed and woollen-headed, my hangover is making itself known. The engines hum, the hours count down. We have flown east through the daytime into early night again, and by the time we cross into Pakistan the cabin lights are dimmed and windows covered. The mood in the aircraft sours as the announcement is made — we are crossing from Pakistan into Kandahar province.

We make our way into Afghanistan like burglars in the night- as silent and unnoticed as we can be. The engine note changes as we descend, and a few hours before dawn we land on the foreign tarmac of Kandahar Airfield, and row by row, are bidden to stand and march off.

Despite being shrouded in night, a blasting heat rises off the runway to meet us. In the floodlit darkness the throng of men splits apart and joins together in our regimental groups. Fijian soldiers from the Logistics Corps unload cargo nets of backpacks and bags, calling to each other and laughing. A forklift rolls along to haul cargo, and an officer arrives to give us a briefing. I find Vince, and we are ushered down concrete steps into a large concrete bunker, dug out of the Afghan ground with foreign picks and shovels. I am already in the belly of the machine, part of an enormous conveyor belt of parts and people.

An RAF officer tells us the base rules, 'You must keep your helmets and body-armour with you at all times, you must take cover immediately if you hear the IDF siren.'

IDF — Indirect fire — are rockets or mortars that the Taliban launch into the base from their hidden firing points deep in the maze of Kandahar city. The reality of where we find ourselves is kicking in. We are to report back to the waiting area at dusk for onward transport to Camp Bastion, in neighbouring Helmand province, which will be under cover of the next night. Stood down, we are shown to a ramshackle Afghan bus, driven by a local, which will take us to a hangar where we can get some sleep.

The bus rattles us around the airfield, passing close by the wire that marks the edge of the camp and the no man's land that stretches from wire through scrubland and stones to the shanty town city that is visible. Kandahar, home to Khans and Moguls of time before, crossroads to The East and the gateway to India, is nestled snug on the hills like an old friend. I can smell her close around us as we drive across potted dirt roads, the fumes of a thousand Soviet era cars her warm breath, the human filth her perfume.

My comrades around me are as fresh faced as I am, new to the country and immersed in thought as we drive across the outskirts of the airfield. The bus lights are on, and we are illuminated. I try and pull the curtains next to me, but they are sewn open. We haven't even been issued weapons yet, and I feel oddly on show. The bus driver, his head wreathed in blue smoke from his cigarette, lurches us to a halt beside a concrete and steel hangar that looks exactly like the previous and exactly like the next. We haul our kit off the bus, and find a hundred empty cot beds laid out in regimental lines inside. Vince and I take bunks next to each other, and we wash our faces and prepare to rest.

◊ ◊ ◊ ◊ ◊

My first night — morning — in Afghanistan is spent in an excited haze, dozing and waking, dreaming I am on the airfield bus again, then lying on my bed and listening to the world wake around me. The day, too, passes like a dream, and before long I am back on the bus in the early evening, rattling back to the hub where we will be corralled and checked off a clipboard, herded into waiting areas, to sit on our backpacks and wait some more. After enough time has passed, Vince and I are put on a Hercules plane, a small, squat ugly thing with the belly slung under the wings. We clamber aboard, clip in and wait. The Hercules lumbers into the air with a roar, and we are away. Like the Russians before us, we cross provinces by air and at night. We are going west, into Helmand Province, the Pashtun heartland and the opium capital of the world, where our regiment is already starting operations against the Taliban. Vince and I are on the last flight into Bastion as we join Operation Herrick 9. We land under cover of darkness into my new home Camp Bastion, and the machine swallows us up.

3.HEAT ON THE RANGES

2nd Battalion the Parachute Regiment are leaving Afghanistan. Their deployment complete, their depleted ranks cluster during the day in their lines, stripped to the waist. Tanned, tattooed, and bored, they are filling their final days in country with weapon cleaning and fitness training. A stone's throw and a spit away, my company are temporarily housed in a Camp Bastion transit tent, a vast single canvas filled with cots and stifled air. We are packed in like sardines, with equipment and men all vying for space. We sweat every hour of day and night, whiling away the few days until the Royal Irish Regiment fly home, leaving company lines for us to fill. My new home is a 6' by 2' cot bed, with barely enough space to heave my hold-all and backpack beneath. Even after living with my comrades cheek-by-jowl these past months the complete intrusion of the army into every aspect of my life grates on my nerves. We sleep so cramped that I could reach out and touch the sleepers on either side, we wash side by side in metal basins, and we sit shoulder to shoulder on wooden benches in the mess hall to eat our daily rations.

We have a few days of test firing our weapons, then tactics lessons and operational handovers by the outgoing brigade. We will start our deployment with joint patrols, and then — finally — the Irish will have left and our duty will properly begin.

◊ ◊ ◊ ◊ ◊

On my third day in country, green as a tourist, puffed and red and sweating, I find myself marching behind a slow-crawling Land Rover out to the ranges. My new armour is fresh from the stores, my rifle is at the trail and the sun's morning pride pricks my eyes. We are creeping out of camp, safely in the midst of a company of men, all as fresh as I. Excitement rises in my chest and splits a smile on my face as we exit the camp, and I take my eyes off the boots of the man in front and look to the horizon. The dirt-packed road and drainage ditches snake away from camp and turn north towards the mountains. In the days and months to come, the shape of each peak will be etched into my mind until the sight of each foreign and far-off peak evokes a familiar longing and comfort. Now, seeing them for the first time in glimpses between trudging boots kicking up dust, the mountains seem foreboding, larger than anything I had thought to see here. There are many miles of plains between us and them, but of these I know and see nothing. Away in the direction of our march, westwards, all I can see are the ranges. Built by ISAF troops, they are shooting galleries made up of machined berms. South, the desert rolls away, sandy and stony, dunes and undulations all the way to the horizon.

The day is a blasting heat, stripped of all moisture by the pitiless sun. Within minutes lips are cracked, throats parched and my tongue fuzzy and dry. The weight of my armour drags my shoulders down into a stoop, and with every footfall sweat beads on the end of the nose to fall and drip onto the dust below. Sweat is racing out of me from head to toe, and though my shirt was clean this morning it is soaked and grimy already. Our boots crunch on oven-baked stones, our column moves forward at a march, and the minutes struggle by as the ranges grow ever nearer.

◊ ◊ ◊ ◊ ◊

We stop short of the ranges, and our escort of Irish Rangers assemble metal detectors and check the firing points for IEDs. We line up, column and row, and at an order the first row moves forward and loads their weapons. At another order, they fire away at the distant targets, then when each has fired enough rounds they stop, unload, and go and check the targets. They adjust their weapon sights with clicks and turns, then another round of firing starts. When enough targets have holes in the right places, they retire to the rear and another row starts all over again.

By the time my row is called forwards, I am all but exhausted. We have marched out, stood, waited in the bright sunlight and we have been baked dry for over an hour. There is no shade, no breeze, no escape. I drop down onto the firing point, tasting acrid cordite in the air, and the weight of my armour taken off my shoulders is a beautiful relief. Mercifully, the firing is short, and my rifle is declared accurate.

◊ ◊ ◊ ◊ ◊

The march back is an ordeal like no other. It is nearly midday, and the searing heat of the morning's march was like a warm summer evening in comparison. Two men stumble and collapse with heat exhaustion, and are hauled into the escort vehicle to have their hands doused in water. One of them had the EWD — electronic warfare device — and I am given it to carry instead. The landscape, exciting and new this morning already seems tired and familiar. We enter the camp, and reach company lines. My newly-accurate rifle is taken from me and locked in the Company Quarter Master (CQM) Serjeant's shipping container, replaced with an unfired light machine gun. I am to be my section's machine gunner, and loaded down with my gun and belts of ammunition, I retire to the shared tent to organise my gear.

My section commander Vince has a new weapon, a grenade launcher slung under his rifle. He has given his rifle a name — Andalucía, which he lisps in Spanish style. He insists that I name my machine gun too. A few Spanish names are offered and rejected, and I settle for Bellaniña. Bella's pistol grip moulds to my hand, her weight is my companion as for the next few days we take lessons in open-air classrooms on language and suicide bombers, the opium economy and the rules of engagement.

We are hungry for our duties, eager, impatient for the Royal Irish to depart and for us to begin making our mark on this province and this country. We were watching the clock, watching the date, and waiting. But the Taliban were watching, too. In the days and months to come, I would see how unforgiving this land can be, go head-to-head with the Taliban bomb makers in a game for our lives, and learn first-hand that in war, no-one comes through unscathed. Herrick 9 was about to begin.

4. SANGAR DUTY

It is my first night of duties in Afghanistan, and I have been given sentry. I am robed in the dim blue light that creeps through the windows of my concrete cave. Surrounded by four bare walls, the sangar's four bare windows are open gashes into the night beyond. I step forward, without enough light to see by I am blindly groping and grasping, weakly flapping to find my bearings by touch. My fingers ahead of me brush something, flesh against rough wood. A table is crouched in front of the forward window, I plant my feet and explore its surface. At first, I find only the smooth tabletop, but there, the palm-sucking grasp of a pistol grip, and here, the warm body of a machine gun, nosing out into the darkness beyond. I run my thumb along the pistol grip. We have never met, but I know the body of this weapon inside and out. I gently caress the raised button I find. It doesn't move, so the safety catch is off and the working parts forward. Is it loaded though? I run my left hand along the belly, feeling the closed dust cover, then stop and raise my hand slowly. A lightly oiled belt of ammunition rises like a cat's purr. The weapon is loaded, to fire all I need to do is cock the weapon, then squeeze off.

My shock-wide, blinking eyes begin to relent and adjust

to the gloom, and the darkness unclenches slowly. Discarded weapon sights show as dark blobs on the table, the detritus of the last sentry scattered around: dead batteries from the night vision sight, empty sausage roll wrappers, a glossy magazine hidden under the official documents, the radio log and range cards. I feel them all, then take control of my new home, and move and adjust and comfort myself in the business of making this sangar mine. Night stag, we call it, or the death stag — named not for the violence of war, but because in the small hours, between three and five in the morning, you will get so tired and depressed that you will wish you were dead.

The heat of the baking desert lingers long into the night, radiating back at me from the concrete bunker. I am two floors up, encased in an RPG-stopping cage, locked and double-locked — the modern ravelin, or sangar, is a miniature fortress. My sangar, on the edge of the airfield of Bastion, is a remote and lonely station. I face east, out into the desert and across the central valley. Behind me the lights of Bastion twinkle in the distance, a kilometre or more away. The airfield is empty, a vast expanse of blackness all around the main landing strip. Away north and south, hundreds of metres away, stand more lonely sangars, distant and aloof. Due to manpower shortages, though, only every other sangar is manned. That makes eight men stretched across a mile of wire which marks the eastern edge of Camp Bastion, two men to a sangar.

I sigh and feel thankful again that we are locked inside, enclosed behind steel and enmeshed safe in our cage. The blackness slackens off as my eyes relax further, and the dim light now shows more of my surroundings in the bunker. I settle down onto the wooden stool pushed behind the gun and begin the long business of watching the desert. Tired but determined, I fix my jaw and force myself to scan the desert with the night vision sight, picking up magnified bushes and hollows in the undulating desert terrain in an artificial green glow. The green image of the desert holds no surprises, just the familiar rolling contours of dunes that will appear in my dreams when I finally sleep after dawn. I take in the shape of the runnels, the darkening of scrubby vegetation in the low ground, and watch for movement; for shapes or shines, silhouettes or shadows that look out of place. I sit and watch as the moon slides under the horizon behind me, unseen, beyond Camp Bastion.

Alone with my thoughts in the comfort of the close warm sangar, the escape of daydream is a powerful lure, and even unbidden my mind starts to enter pre-sleep relaxation. I exhale away a layer of consciousness and watch out into the desert. The night moves on towards dawn, and finally my night's duty is done.

5. SMITH AND CHRIS AT THE EFI

We move into our new lines a few days later, a camp within a camp, a weather-beaten row of shipping containers boxing in a dozen tents, lined out along walkways of interlocked plastic matting. Our new streets quickly acquire names of home; we have North Hill, and Wyvern Way.

My tent is the first on North Hill, which I share with half of 2 Platoon. We sleep on cotbeds, our backpacks and holdalls stored beside, and for privacy we hang ponchos and shemaghs from cord to divide down our sleeping area from the next soldier's. The tent is dark at all hours, light coming through the thick canvas from the entrance flap. We have strip lights overhead but they are rarely used, as there are always men on night duties, or men between taskings grabbing an hour of sleep here and there.

My shemagh is draped over my eyes, I loll on my cotbed and I am drifting on the verge of sleep; I know nothing of Smith slipping his way into my bedspace until he whips the shemagh off. Beautiful sleep, so close, vanishes and I grimace and squint up at the figure looming over me.

'Addy, Chris is going to be at the EFI after O-Group. He's off to his FOB tomorrow, want to come and have a tin of coke?'

I didn't think we'd see the big brother of our platoon until he came back through camp for Rest and Recuperation in January. I groan my assent, and Smith waves a pack of cards at me, the unspoken question answered with another groan from me. I wriggle my feet into combat boots kept beside the bed, laces tied but open wide enough to slip on should I need to respond to an attack quickly. Smith saunters to the brew station at the entrance to my tent. We are lucky in my tent, as we have one electric socket and a kettle, and enough cotbeds that all ten of us get one and no-one has to sleep on the floor. Smith brings back an enormous mug full of steaming noodles, with two disposable forks sticking out. Welfare packages from the anonymous well-wishers arrive in dribs and drabs, to be rationed out at random. We've had a women's group in Exeter adopt us as their honorary unit, and although stores may be for storing, the women's group are quite happy to do their bit for the war effort. Thanks to their care packages we have amassed a good two score of instant noodles, various hard sweets, soaps and toothpaste, and the occasional magazine designed to cater to male tastes from the more liberal minded women. The lucky recipients tear out the best pages to stick up by their beds to keep morale up. The welfare package I opened last contained a fishing magazine instead, and my bedspace is now decorated with double-page folds of enormous carp, voluptuous and green. Close ups of tails and scales wink down at me between alluring (but tasteful) pages of plugs and spinners for sea bass and mackerel.

Smith's noodles are cooling as he settles down into a folding chair in the centre of the tent, and deals a pack of camouflage deck cards into the customary hands. I grab a wooden stool made from pallet planks by a soldier long-home and settle down for the serious business at hand. Hands swap between cards, passing the mug between us, and forkfuls of noodles, as we play the time away until O-Group. Hands are dealt and lost and re-dealt, and our fortunes wax and wane until we have both lost and won and lost count.

As night steals in, we cannot delay O-Group any longer, and Smith riffles the cards back into an ammunition pouch. We collect our weapons to make the march over to the admin tent, where the nightly briefing is about to start.

◊ ◊ ◊ ◊ ◊

The O-Group is the briefing from our platoon commander. He rattles off the items on his list whilst we scribble notes. Tonight's items: we have to wear our headgear at all time outside of lines, as there's a General visiting from Kandahar in a few days, and a reminder to take anti-malarials daily. The boss rattles through a few more items.

'Last 24 hours — rocket attack at Kandahar. No casualties.' He looks around to make sure we are all paying attention. 'Possible suicide IED vehicle attack being planned around Marjah. Might be in a red or possibly white Toyota.'

Jacobs snorts. 'Not much to go on, is it?'

The boss takes this personally. 'Something funny about this briefing? This is to keep you lot safe, so switch on and screw the nut, or you'll be on stag from now until the end of tour. Got it?' The boss looks down at the next item on his briefing notes. He looks up. 'Female beggar, large build' he announces to us. Then he looks down again to find the next item.

Vince's brow furrows as he takes this in. 'Sir, what about the beggar?'

The boss frowns. 'Doesn't say… Female beggar, large build. Now then, Serjeant Barney has drawn up a new duty list, we've got to back-fill some duties that 1st Battalion need, so some of you are going to FOB Tombstone for a week or so. Anyone got anything for me? Right, over to Serjeant Barney then.'

Somehow all this takes twenty minutes, and as usual my eyes glaze over long before the end. After Serjeant Barney takes five minutes to re-iterate what has already been said, we are dismissed to our duties. My next duty is sentry on sangar the following day, so in my evening's admin time Smith and I lug our weapons over to the EFI at the allotted time to see Chris.

◊ ◊ ◊ ◊ ◊

It's a twenty-minute walk across camp, and by the time we reach the EFI — a steel fabricated building the size of a shearing shed — the dusk has moved into full-blown night, crickets are sounding in the blackness outside the yellow glare of electric lanterns, and we arrive to find a throng of soldiers already sitting cramped on wooden benches around wooden tables in the outside air.

We make our way inside a packed EFI building; FOBS have not yet changed out fully, so the troops are a mix of off-going and in-coming soldiers. We push our way around the packed tables, and find a place in the queue at the bar, waiting our turn by a pair of Lancers who are swearing and jeering at each other, goading and joking to pass the time. When our turn arrives, I order a coke and pay in crisp dollar bills, with cardboard discs handed back as change. Coins are too heavy to transport in and out of Afghanistan by air, so the US army has come up with its own currency 'freedom cents', printed on cardboard with encouraging slogans like 'OOH-RAH' and 'OEF: OPERATION ENDURING FREEDOM' screaming out in bold print emblazoned on each one.

Cokes in hand, the first test is passed. Now we will find Chris, or somewhere to sit. We move a few laps of the EFI building without seeing Chris, so we must wait and let him find us. We try to squeeze onto benches outside. Luck is on our side, for a section of Parachute Regiment troops are hefting their weapons and clearing a bench as we near, and Smith and I plonk down quickly. My coke is half empty when Chris sidles up, meandering amongst the soldiers and airmen crowding the tables, and announces himself with an imitation of a bugle call, 'Doo da do daaahhh.'

We shift and sit and settle, craning to hear over the chatter drifting into the night sky, as Chris tells us about his new platoon and his tasking. He's part of the OMLT team, training the ANA to fight their own battles by leading from the front and showing how it's done. They have been on the ranges for night-shoots, and the next day are heading out to Garmsir. We linger as the darkness around us deepens and the night chill sits on our shoulders like a blanket, talking about the good times and the better times, laughing until our stomachs ache and our cheeks are numb. We are lost for a while in a happy bubble of our own, until time like a rising tide can be held back no longer and with a glance at a watch reality must bite back, and the bubble is gone. It is time to head back to our bunks. We rise and fare-well and turn.

Chris gives us some last advice before he goes, 'Always, always, get in your time machine whenever you can — sleeping makes the tour go quicker! I'll see you boys again when I'm through for R&R. Tell Eski from me he's a blower.' And with those words of wisdom, Chris is gone into the blackness, like the chatter from a hundred soldiers drifting into the swirling night air — close, but out of reach.

◇ ◇ ◇ ◇ ◇

We plod back to lines around the ditch edges, with Danish armoured vehicles rumbling past us on the dusty roads and a helicopter engine roaring on the flight line. The soft crunch of our boots on the dirt marks time, and we march around Hesco walls, bypassing camps within camps, heading for our time machine sleeping bags and the new day.

6. THE DESERT PATROLS

Finally, I am out of camp, out on the ground, in the vast area of operations codenamed 'Robin', the largest in Helmand. Now, everything is new, every dune and hidden valley springing into view from the desert is seen for the first time. My face is creased in a permanent grin of excitement as we race across the desert in dusty patrol after patrol, eager to fight, ready to find the enemy.

Our vehicle patrol is only six men in two vehicles, mostly Riflemen, the highest ranking a Lance Corporal. We rise in silence before dawn, and without a word, dress, wash, line up at the urinals, then haul our kit to the vehicle yard. The yard is an enclosure made up of shipping containers on the inside of one of the many roads looping around the camp. The night patrol is already here for handover, dusty and happy. A wind-up FM radio plays on the bonnet of a WMIK, and they restock the vehicles with batteries, water, refuel and check the radios. We take control, I climb onto the outside of my WMIK, clambering over struts and onto the turret, to drop inside the back. Jacobs, the other top cover, hands me up Bella and my daysack. A WMIK is a stripped-down Land Rover, with a cage in the back holding a 360-degree mobile turret, and ballistic panels strapped on to protect the top cover. Safely inside, I recheck the batteries on every piece of kit, and check we have enough for eighteen hours run time. My daysack is placed to my side on the floor, flap open, with grab-bag on top stuffed with eight hundred rounds for my machine gun, and my grenades. Bella, propped in the corner, is lightly oiled and wrapped in a shemagh to keep the dust off her. Batteries are lined up with the metal detector strapped on top. I check the flares, breakdown kit, spare fuel cans. A quick count shows all my boxed rounds of 7.62mm bullets are accounted for. The radio is switched on, working, and tuned to the correct frequency. I check the electronic warfare devices are working normally, then to the gun, my GPMG mounted in the turret. I check the gun is oiled and clean, has a full lateral traverse, rises and falls easily. We are nearly ready. The remainder of the crew are immersed in their own handover routine. My turret ready, I jump out and wait by the Hesco wall of the work yard, sharing a battered roll-up cigarette with Jacobs whilst the oncoming and offgoing patrol commanders exchange notes.

When the last man has stowed the last bit of kit and all the vehicles are ready to face the day, we mount up again. I clamber onto the rear wheel, grab a strut, and haul my armour-laden body up over the side of the gun turret and plonk down. I check the radio codes for the day one last time, then take post, standing with my head and shoulder protruding from the gun turret, manning a GPMG, stock in my shoulder and one hand in my pocket. Engines bark into life, and the wagons cough and roll their way across the umber roads of camp towards the main gate.

◊ ◊ ◊ ◊ ◊

Our unit has been given a mix of tasks. We might be clearing the high-risk area around the airfield to prevent the departing flights taking anti-aircraft fire. Other days and nights we patrol Highway One, the concrete road connecting Gereshk to the east of our AO with the western province of Nimruz. We might stop and search vehicles, to try and find smuggled weapons or opium. Sometimes we are given a compass point: east, north, south, or west, and we are to patrol to the edge of our AO to show our presence to locals and deny the enemy freedom of movement. One multiple at a time will be on immediate notice to move, with the IRT — incident response team — and will scramble to a Chinook when a call comes through, to fly out to a casualty and extract them back for medical treatment. In the fighting season that comes, the IRT will be called out every day.

When we are not patrolling and not on IRT duty, we are on sentry around the camp or in FOB Tombstone, the outpost camp to the west of Bastion where the Afghan National Army have a detachment of commanders planning their operations in Helmand. Helicopter flights and convoys have already left Camp Bastion to take the fighting units to their FOBs around the province. 3 Commando Brigade are back, and like every unit from every army before, we mean to finish the job we came to do.

7. LOOKING OUT OVER NAD ALI

We have patrolled out to the edges of the plateau, and from here steep slopes dive away into a wide valley: a wadi (the word is borrowed from Arabic), carved out of the sandstone by immeasurable volumes of water over aeons of time. Across the other side of the valley — no, the other side of the wadi —the hills rise up to plateau again, the mirror image of the plain Camp Bastion sits upon. Hummocks and hillocks mark the boundary, and down in the bed of the wadi, a vast expanse kilometres wide, small farmstead compounds have sprung up, haze clinging to them in the cool morning light. Dusty ochre is dashed with grey as far as the eye can see, save for the dirt track scoured into the wadi by vehicles' passing, a child's imitation of the scour that cut the wadi all those years ago.

Binoculars and weapon sights are brought to bear, and we survey the few cars bumping their way slowly down the wadi, north to south. We snake our way even slower southwards, clinging to the hilltops. As we rattle and creak our way along the patrol route, the wadi opens like a welcoming door, showing us the town of Nad Ali. There is a canal running east–west which forms the town limits, the edge of our AO. By the time we would reach the canal we would be deep inside a dense sprawl of compounds — the outskirts of the town, a maze of dirt roads snaking around blocks of mud brick houses and smaller and smaller field systems. There is no ISAF presence in Nad Ali, the edge of the AO is marked red on the map: 'FLET' —Forward Line, Enemy Troops. It is Taliban held, far outside our control (admittedly so), for even the areas notionally under our control are contested by violence and constantly being won and re-won. But for Nad Ali, there is no such ambiguity. It is enemy territory, from here through Babaji and Marjah districts, and not until you reach Lashkar Gah does the 'FLET' give way to 'FLOT' — Forward Line, Own Troops.

Nad Ali is green and grey — the green of the Green Zone. The Helmand River winds through it, and from the reverse adits of irrigation canals, waters diffuse out to bring a lush growth of trees, grasses, crops and shrubs. From this distance the green splashes of colour wind around a landscape almost unchanged for centuries. The townscape is grey from buildings and buildings again, low mud compounds too many to count fill the town to the horizon, mosque domes ease their way higher in the sky, and everywhere the town teems with activity. Distant figures walk the roads, cars rattle in and out of sight, smoke rises from chimneys and the river runs through it all. The sights are vivid, exotic, hinting of the Silk Road of years past, of an unknown, impossibly different world from that which we have known so far.

◊ ◊ ◊ ◊ ◊

We follow the hillsides at the side of the wadi, edging closer to Nad Ali, an overt patrol. The morning mist clings only to low ground the sunlight has not yet found, and our vehicles on the hillsides overlooking the town will be visible for miles around. I wonder how many binoculars — weapon sights, even — will be trained on us today, gauging these new troops, seeing how we work, how we think, how we react, anticipating how the next six months will unfold. I wonder the same myself, as we watch the town, and the town watches back.

8. THE MOUNTAINS & VEHICLE HANDOVER

The mountains stand tall and proud, high up to the north, a wall of jutting rock lifted from the desert to stretch to the clear blue sky. Haze covers the horizon to their base, the stony desert eked out for miles between us and them. From Nad Ali, the canal, and the southern edges of AO Robin, they disappear behind a veil, seeming impossibly faint to our naked eyes, searching and straining in the harsh, bright light. From Bastion or the wadis they are in full view and punctuate the skyline like a memorable cityscape, each shape and shoulder. There, the twins, away on the west side pointing the way to FOB Juno. And there, the pyramid, the north marker with a jagged, pointed capstone summit. They were invisible when we flew in; first seen on the morning when we marched out to the ranges and everything was new and exciting. Now, they soothe us with their presence, and each northern patrol we take onto the sand and grist plateau they rise from is an easy, comforting ride.

There are few farms and compounds up north, and better visibility. The heart-racing panic of getting bogged down in the mud fields of the southern villages fades to a casual impatience in the shadow of the mountains. They stood, tall and proud, as the USSR rushed troops in, for them to die in thousands. They stood when Jalalabad fell, when the British of old played 'The Great Game' and occupied this space. Troops before us rolled the dice, came and went, with flood and ebb. And now they stand over us. Tomorrow, we will sleep and still they will stand.

We have patrolled the wadi from midnight, and the pyramid has turned from a dark shadow into her familiar daytime self by the time we return. We park up by Wyvern lines. Jacobs jumps out of his vehicle and drops his daysack on the ground, resting his rifle atop and away from the floor, with his helmet balanced on top to protect it from wind-blown dust. He unclips his radio headset and pulls it away, letting the fresh air cool him. I do the same in the Vector beside him, stowing Bella then pulling my shemagh from her and wrapping it about my head to keep the sun off. We will be here for close to an hour, seeing to the vehicles then handing them over to 1 Platoon. First, we have to make them ready and replenish the supplies.

Jacobs climbs back into the WMIK next to me and changes the High Frequency (HF) radio to today's midday frequency, then he clambers onto the turret and passes me the torn notebook page with Vince's biro scribbles on it telling me the new code. I lean out of the Vector top cover hatch, stretching to reach it, then drop down inside the Vector and retune our radio set. I call Jacobs on the HF set as a radio check, but he's already on his way to pick up batteries, and a sentry in a front gate sanger answers my radio check instead.

We took over the vehicles just over twelve hours ago, and have run down their fuel, drained their radio batteries, changed batteries on the EWD every few hours and now have armfuls of empty cells to be recharged. I pick up a pair of them, heavy electronic bricks in olive green, and lug them past tents and through our lines to the shed where the company signaller keeps a constant supply of fresh batteries, dropping them on the 'to be charged' desk. It takes three trips to restock the batteries, and another two to pick up fresh water from our Quartermaster to replace what has been drunk or handed out to locals on our last patrol.

I took over the Vector from Flint, one of the Bloody Eleventh from another platoon and a friend. His Vector was well kept when I stepped inside before midnight, and I intend to return the compliment, making sure I give back the armoured vehicle in the best condition.

Nikky the motor pool Rifleman has brought fuel, and the drivers and vehicle commanders have finished refuelling, a pair of them apiece tipping giant jerrycans to fill the thirsty tanks again. With the fuel safety stowed, we are allowed to smoke outside the vehicles and Jacobs sits on the edge of the WMIK gun turret, rolling a pair of cigarettes. He throws one to Litch, who sparks up and tosses a lighter in return. Nikky offers me a drag from his Afghan cigarette, and I take it thankfully, sucking a deep lungful and feeling the familiar nicotine buzz race through me. I hand it back, and take out a heavy-bristled paintbrush from my rifle cleaning kit and dust off the GPMGs, uncoil 7.62mm link from the ammo boxes and blow off the desert dust, then re-coil it again.

We used the Vallon a few times at choke points, stored in the Vector but operated by Jacobs, and I dust it down and re-box it. The rations box has been depleted too, and another journey into company lines to the Quartermaster's office sees me picking up fresh ration packs for the next patrol. Finally, my handover admin is complete and I sit in the back of the Vector, legs dangling out the rear doors, whilst the drivers and commanders prepare their patrol report and handover paperwork.

1 Platoon have started to arrive, and Flint joins me in the back of the Vector, his squinting face creased into his trademark permanent smile. We exchange greetings and I hand over to him, letting him know about the farmers' guard dogs running loose around compound Blue 44, the flatbed truck we stopped with three poppy farmers inside, who turned out to be moving cans of diesel for their generators. He takes it all in, the account of the atmosphere, the reactions from the locals, the movements and interactions; the Pashtun pattern of life that we are coming to know more and more. He shrugs when I complete my mini-patrol report.

'Doesn't matter today, we're headed north. But good to know for future.'

'Any news from home?' I ask. Flint has his eye set on a girl he met during build up training — they've been exchanging letters. He knows what I'm really asking and smiles, wolfish and secretive.

'Ah well, she's only human. I'll get there.'

I'm sure he will. The uniform and the deployment are an easy, ready-made backstory and identity, and the girls of Exeter love a soldier; there had been many sweethearts made during our forays into town.

Handover gone from my mind now, I think back to weeks past, and home. Like Flint, I had my eye set on a girl too. Perhaps it was expected, that a soldier has a sweetheart to write to whilst he's away? Maybe I was playing the role I was given, going through the motions, caught up in the tragic idea of love and separation and a soldier's duty. Maybe I wanted something else to replace the loneliness I had been carrying around since my civilian days, and my life before my life before this one. Whatever it was, and to my surprise, with the false confidence my uniform gave me the girl had become my girlfriend just before we deployed to Afghanistan.

'How's Charlotte?' Flint asks suddenly, but I wave the

question away, embarrassed. At Shorncliffe in Kent after another live fire exercise, I got drunk with Smith and asked him to be best man when I married her, Charlotte, this girl I hardly knew. The idea died when morning and sobriety came, but after that I was Addy, the soldier who'd marry anyone after two beers.

The commanders and drivers have handed over now, and as Flint clambers to his gun I pass him his Minimi machine gun and daysack, then heave my kit onto a shoulder and set off towards my tent. Jacobs sings softly, soulfully as we walk, 'Ain't no sunshine when she's gone', and I harmonise with him, deep bass chords rumbling in my throat, as Jacobs goes through his own motions of love and separation, singing about any one of the many girls he left behind when we boarded the ride that brought us here.

9. GREEN BALLS

We have been waiting for their helicopter for several hours now, lounging on our vehicles as the dusk slides into night and the mosquitoes slowly stop buzzing. Night's chill comes quicker, and sleeves are rolled down, shemaghs gathered about necks, and cigarettes sparked to keep the cold at bay. We are at FOB Tombstone, waiting for a number of officers to arrive via Chinook from inspecting their FOBs in Kajaki. Our task is to escort them back to Bastion in a pair of vehicles, a Vector and a Vixen Land Rover. Minutes of wait have turned into hours, and they are late.

As suddenly as they are late, rotor blades appear to our ears, a steady whomp-whomp-whomp building and growling until the air is thick with noise, the dust is whipped up, and an enormous Chinook settles and bounces down just ahead of the gate, on Shorabak HLS.

Four uniformed, armoured shades stride towards us, and as they come closer the breeze brings an unmistakable smell, mingled with aviation fuel from the Chinook and tobacco from our patrol. Perfume! The group stops just inside the gate, the CO of 1st Battalion Rifle Regiment is here to discuss handover with them. By the orange light of the walkway lamps, we can see a pair of men, tall and imposing, leading the group but also a pair of shorter, differently proportioned soldiers standing back. Admin officers or medics, or one of each. Female, blonde. Just how we like them.

Conlay whistles softly. 'Bugger me, it's birds.'

The bored semi-silence of a few minutes ago gives way to filthy streams of full-blown innuendo and excitement. The women's perfume has reminded us of the comforts of home, of civilisation, and within a few weeks some of us will again be sampling the normal pleasures that we took for granted, as R&R flights will be starting.

Vince calls across the patrol, 'Chaps with me, birds in the Snatch.' Meaning the men will travel in the Vector with him, the women will be — they'll be in my vehicle!

He calls up to me, 'Hey Addy, think you'll be able to handle a pair of them?' I have a wide grin on my face.

Chalky laughs. He regales us with a story about transporting a civilian woman in Ireland, and how the top cover put a glow stick down his pants, dangling his glowing crotch in her face whilst standing on top cover, and the poor woman's embarrassment. We all laugh.

'I'll give that a go,' I say.

'Hey Vince, Addy's going to give them the glowing bollock treatment. Just keep your trousers on Addy!'

I duck down into my Vixen, and fumble around with a glow stick, cracking a pair and shaking them until the green glow shines bright, and then stowing them down my boxers. I stick my head through the top cover hatch, facing rearwards, Bella in my shoulder. Now all I need to do is wait. Behind me, at the head of the patrol, I hear Vince introducing himself to our transports.

'This way please.'

Feet approach. I give one final waggle to the glow stick down my pants. The CO and RSM of a Guards Regiment clamber into the back of my vehicle. My groin, at eye level, is glowing bright green. Vince smiles at me as he shows the female admin officers to his Vector. Furious, the RSM glares. Am I trying to make a fool of him?!

The drive back to Bastion seems to take an age. We roll through the gate, and turn left instead of right, taking the scenic route. Vince is clearly enjoying himself, and in no hurry to drop our passengers off. Eventually, though, his fun comes to an end, as our vehicle convoy reaches its destination.

As I close the doors behind our departing transports, Vince's voice breaks over the radio. 'Well, they were a lovely pair. Keen to get to know a young infantry NCO. How were your passengers, Addy?'

10. DHOBI-WALLAH

Dhobi-wallah's shack sits at the junction halfway between our lines and the lines holding the Queen's Dragoon Guards. Every few days, when warm, wet socks smell like ammonia, and every shirt you wear has stuck to your back with sweat at least twice, we bundle up our small clothes into white net bags issued one per man. In go the thick black woollen socks, the clinging black boxer shorts sewn through with metallic strands of silver, the spare shirt and spare combat trousers, and off we heave to the wooden shed of washers and dryers, to Dhobi-wallah. Dhobi-wallah has one job, laundry, and his cabin is awash with ledgers and sheets of paper, all scribbled with net numbers and names and times and dates, mystically ordered so that he can magically lose your washing and try to give you someone else's.

Conlay and I trudge with weapons slung across our backs, carrying five nets per man. We crunch across the dirt, and rattle across plastic matting walkways, snaking our way around company lines and work yards. A General and an MP are visiting, so we all have to have our regimental belts on our combat trousers, our regimental beret atop our heads, and regimental faces freshly shaven.

We reach Dhobi-wallah. Conlay and I hand over our bags, and reach for the papers to scrawl our names and units and the names of our comrades, date, net numbers, shoe size and divide it by the first number we thought of. Then, Dhobi-wallah ignores his system and throws all the nets into random washers, shooing us away with his hand, all broad smiles and shy words in his own language.

On the way back to our lines, I leave Conlay at the junction where the satellite phone antenna and dish sits behind barbed wire.

'I'll see you back at lines mate.'

I queue up again, this time for the telephone and a crackled call to my girlfriend Charlotte, to hear about life back in Plymouth, about office politics and weather, and I try and force myself to be cheerful. Before the end of the call, I am weary of the pretence, and am itching to get back to lines to get some sleep before I change onto vehicle patrol later that night. We say goodbye, and the line crackles and dies.

11. NAD ALI OUTSKIRTS

We patrolled out in a pair of WMIKs as the call to prayer drifted high into the dawn sky. Down in the wadis and beside Highway One, the few cars stopped where they were, and prayer mats were placed down by freshly cleaned hands. Whilst the faithful prayed, we moved south. The wadi opened up and compounds dashed the landscape ever thicker, and still we pushed on. Field systems are passed by, flocks and herds, farms and villages, barely stirring in the first light of a new day. As we near the canal and the bridge into Nad Ali, the boss spins us south west, and we follow the line of the town. The boss rarely patrols with us, but today he is in the lead vehicle and he wants to gauge the locals' attitudes. This means we are heading south into the outer sprawl of Nad Ali.

I hunker over my GPMG mount, goggles down against the biting wind. I am in the rear vehicle, but I am facing out to the flank of our patrol. Behind me are the hills of the wadi edge, far into the distance, but my gun is trained towards the compounds we are skirting, watching for any trouble. I

53

cannot see where we are going, and perhaps that is a good thing. I much prefer the wide expanse of desert, of the mountains of the north or the remote village of the western wadi Bedouins. Here, everywhere you look is a potential firing point, an ambush point, an enemy hiding in plain sight.

We are attracting attention now, figures in doorways follow us with their eyes, children stop and stand still to watch us pass. Compounds to both sides of us now, and we weave through fields and over dykes, following the boss's whim. My palm is sweat-streaked on the gun whilst my mind buzzes in overdrive. I am mentally checking ranges to compounds — 200m, 400m, this one 100m — so if there is a contact I will respond quickly and accurately with 7.62mm fire from my machine gun. As I am ranging compounds, I am also keeping an eye on the locals.

What can I see now? What is the atmosphere telling me? Why can't I see his hands? What is she holding? What if he is a suicide bomber? What if this motorcycle doesn't stop? What if? What if?

Hundreds of possibilities are visualised, and then discarded, each one ending with me bringing my weapon to bear and squeezing the trigger in short, accurate bursts to destroy the threat. The top cover's job is to see all these possibilities and then, if one of them starts to unfurl itself, to respond decisively and quickly. Hesitation can mean death, so anticipation and pre-decision are my companions for as long as I stand hour after every hour at my gun mount, rattling our way through the deserts and villages.

We have pushed on almost to the edge of the AO. We are in the outskirts of Nad Ali, and the boss stops us on the dirt track leading out of town and to the western wadi. My vehicle perches on a hillock beside the road, back facing to the hills and guns overlooking the town, whilst the boss's

WMIK crosses the dirt and closes up to the nearest compound. He dismounts the WMIK, and the Afghan interpreter Aziz goes with him. I feel safer now that we are stopped; with the gun platform static it is easier to watch the ground ahead of us, easier to fire from, easier to gauge our surroundings without them constantly changing. This is a paper shield though, as the longer we are stopped, the longer we are at risk. Word will be spreading that we are here, and as the minutes creep by I feel a rising anxiety to be rid of this place and back on the move again. The boss is standing in front of a compound talking to the owner, a short man with a greasy black beard and tan tunic.

Finally, exhaustingly, the boss finishes and returns to the WMIK, and the driver guns the motor. The wheels spin — they have driven into a square, empty patch of dirt that will next spring be used to grow crops. It is well irrigated by an adit that feeds into the canal, and the wheels are spinning in the soft wet dirt. They stop, a crunch comes rattling out of the engine, differential lock engaged, and again the motor runs high, but still the wheels only spin, sinking the WMIK ever deeper into the wheel-cut gouges that marked our arrival. The driver tries to rock them out, reverse gear, now forward gear, now reverse again. Still, mud spitting up from the wheels is the only result. Chatter comes over the radio, and the top cover and the boss clamber out. We are going to pull them out with a towing strop, and my WMIK creeps closer whilst the vehicles commanders choke a pair of strops together and lash them around tow points.

As they work, I watch over the patrol, GPMG cocked and safety off, pointing toward the highest threat I can see, the nearest compounds ahead. Groups of Afghans cluster in dribs and drabs, and more start appearing to see what the commotion is about.

We pull them out at the third attempt, and relief washes over me as we turn tail and power into the hills towards Bastion, leaving me watching back over the town of Nad Ali until it fades from view.

12. HUNTING ROCKETS

We slowly roll up to the cookhouse, cracking the dusty arid pebbles of the desert as the drivers ease engines into rest. The shadows of the advancing evening swirl in my periphery, and a crescent moon swinging overhead catches my attention, and for a moment I am left behind as my friends laugh and tramp towards full bellies.

The moon hangs at, to my foreign eye, an over-skewed angle, her soft glow showing up strange southern stars. Seeing this fresh moon in a strange sky, gazing blandly down like since before time, reminds me of more homely skies, familiar angles of wax and wane, and everything that spins beneath her back home. The moon, high in the sky here, must barely be rising at home. My thoughts race to Charlotte — and the familiar question that far-away lovers ask. Where is she right now? What is she doing? Is she thinking of me? The moment is broken by another vehicle pulling up beside me, and I lope to catch up with my patrol.

We queue for our meal, in long lines of desert-coloured

uniform stretching out of the cookhouse and back along the surrounding plastic mesh walkways. With a bored, thoughtless patience we trickle up to the hot plate.

We eat in silence, though the mess-hall clamours, and I throw down my rice without a care. We have to get back to the wagons soon, so I rise, take my leave, and stalk the length of the tent, side-hipping my way past officers grouped in social clusters in the walkway. Outside, the warm embrace of the early night clings to me, and I am anonymous again, a relief after the cold, bright air-conditioned mess-hall. I clamber into the Vector and haul my armour and ammunition close to hand. I sit at the rear of the vehicles, underneath my closed top cover hatch, beside radios and electronic boxes, snug in my metal-framed seat. Bellaniña rests on my lap.

I am content again in this dark womb, alone, waiting for my comrades to saunter up after their meal and raise the Vector with the familiar din of soldiers joking and laughing. For now though, my isolation is an escape and I relax, stretching my legs out and closing my eyes. A minute or two later, doors click open and bodies jump in. I sit up, stretching and pulling my cheeks to shake off my drowsiness.

'Is Addy there?' says Andy from the front, leaning back. Yawning, I catch his eye, and he laughs. 'Alright sleeping beauty,' he says in his broad Cornish drawl, 'what are you waiting for, breakfast in bed?'

I laugh, wide awake now, and we have to check kit whilst Bazza does a quick head count, and within another minute we're ready to go again.

◊ ◊ ◊ ◊ ◊

Before we move off, I pass the radio headset and handset from my seat forward to Bazza, who takes over control of the comms as patrol commander. As I do so, the radio crackles into life.

'Granite 64, Granite Zero. Contact IDF. Move to my location now, over.'

The message is a brutal stab into our peaceful, red, basking glow inside the Vector. Life flows through our veins, doors slam, voices shout, engines roar amidst the commotion then purr as we speed away. The word 'contact' is only used on the radio when there is some kind of enemy action: either a shooting, a bombing, or in this case, IDF which means the camp is under attack by Taliban rockets or mortars.

◊ ◊ ◊ ◊ ◊

My heart pounds, and with each bump and jolt I rattle around in my seat in the back of the wagon, wedged as I am between the radio boxes and electronic devices. From my webbing kit I pull out a trail of 5.56mm link, and feed it into Bella's feed tray. 'Load,' I call to myself softly, and giggle nervously. I call out to Bazza in the front but he's saying something into the radio handset. I try again. 'What's going on? I didn't hear any rounds land, no explosions or anything.'

He calls back, 'We're just going to find out now.' Then he grabs a map from the dashboard and examines it, stabbing furiously with his finger and saying something to Andy.

From the back of the Vector I can see nothing of the outside world, unless I stand at either of the two machine guns to the front or rear hatches, and throw my body into the night air. My thoughts race, as I wait in the back for orders to man my gun. I assume that we're going back out into the desert, hunting baseplates with the patrol already out, or racing up and across the wadi to cut off the escape route of any mortar team still on the ground out there. The hunters or the cut-off group, which will we be?

In my excitement I can barely sit still. This will be my first action, my first taste of the savageries of the front line in a direct contact. I am sure that we will see the enemy, even though the waning moon shows little and we have no night vision equipment. I do not doubt that the British Army will, once provoked, prove itself to be invincible, omniscient, and we shall save the day and kill those who dared to attack our camp by night. What else are we here for?

The Vector stops and I climb up to get out of the back, and join the fight.

Andy calls to me from the front, 'Ease up there Addy, we're at the Ops room, Bazza is getting orders then we'll be going out.'

I sit back down again, impatiently flicking the carry handle on Bella down and up again. Five minutes pass, and my adrenaline high ebbs away. The night traffic rumbles around us, occasional US Humvees and armoured Cougars whir past on the dusty roads into Bastion 2. I stand up to stick my head out of the top cover hatch, tightening and adjusting my armour as I do so.

Bazza returns and the slam of his door shows his mood. Andy calls back for me to hold on, and as I do so we finally roll towards the main gate. We reach the camp's orbital road, but instead of ploughing straight on and out of the camp, we turn and drive around the inside edge of the camp perimeter, passing under the shadows of sangars. I duck down back inside the Vector.

'Where are we going?' I call to Bazza.

He calls back, 'Rounds landed in camp. Gotta find the blinds. Somewhere near the hospital.'

I hear the words, but it seems so crazy that I don't understand at first. 'But what about the baseplate? We should be out there on the ground. When are we going out?'

Bazza spins around in his seat, and I can see on his face that he's livid but holding his anger in check. 'Addy, we find the blinds, then we'll see what happens.'

Blinds are rounds that landed but did not explode, so there are live mortars or rockets somewhere in the camp.

But still, this is a job for engineers or bomb disposal crews. We should be hunting the enemy fighters who launched the attack, not cleaning up after them. I lean my helmet on the shell of the Vector and close my eyes, blowing out a breath, then sit back down.

We arrive at the hospital, where nurses are clustering outside and clucking like hens. No-one knows where the rounds fell, no-one heard explosions but several nurses say they heard a bang somewhere between the hospital and the edge of camp, which would have been the mortar rounds landing and digging in, if they didn't explode. Armoured up and kitted out with our weapons, I feel foolish standing silently by, waiting for orders, but Bazza is talking with the nurses to find out our search area. A minute later he comes back.

'Check around your wagons, then we'll go down to the junction and sweep upwards.'

I turn around and stamp back to the wagon, pick up a torch out of my pouches and start looking for the impact site. Red and white torchlights sweep back and forth between the two wagons, as we search the ground.

◊ ◊ ◊ ◊ ◊

We're just moving towards the fence, when an officer of engineers runs up with some sappers beside him and starts taking over, barking orders and summoning us back towards him. We are stood down from the search for the time being as the two groups stand around on the road, waiting for orders. Bazza and the officer argue for a while, then Bazza comes back to our group.

'The officer of engineers is taking over the search. Do what they tell you.' He's not angry anymore, just resigned, though he pronounces 'officer' like a swear word.

I get cordon duty, and take post on the main road, to stop any vehicles from coming into the search area. What happens behind me is no concern, so I check around where

I'm standing to make sure I'm not guarding the impact site itself, then settle myself down for a long haul of cordon.

The night wears on. Vehicles drive up; although I am semi-illuminated by the dipped sidelights, I signal them with my torch to slow down, and turn them around whilst the search continues. Thoughts of patrolling out have disappeared; all that remains is the weary resignation of standing sentry on the cordon. Teams criss-cross and sweep and counter-sweep and nothing can be found.

Finally, in the small hours, a shout goes up. A small crater has been found on the outside of the main road, over the drainage ditch. It's not a mortar, it's a 107mm rocket, a large grey-green device half buried in the crater. I am called in from my cordon position, but we are not done for the night. We have to keep sentry duty on the UXO until morning when an ATO — Ammunition Technical Officer, a bomb disposal expert — will get called out to blow the find. The engineers have disappeared; sentry on UXO in camp is beneath them, we're infantry so we get the job.

We stand around the find in a group, deciding on the stag list, and then park the Vector by the crater and illuminate it with our headlights. Watching over the rocket, no-one can get near without us seeing them, so we settle down to watch. I draw first watch, with Cooper. We have four hours before we will be relieved, but it's a struggle to keep my eyes open. I'm not used to sitting down in a Vector, usually I stand on top cover, so the luxury of the soft seat and warm interior coax me into drowsiness. I fight it with all my will, biting my tongue, then stabbing my leg with a pencil to keep myself awake. I look at my watch frequently. Just after four in the morning, the Snatch arrives with Bazza and Richards, and Cooper and I are driven back to our lines.

I sleep whilst I can, but before long I am woken to go back and watch over the rocket again. I'm still on sentry with Flint when the ATO arrives to blow up the rocket, so I stay to see the show. The ATO has an engineer fill sandbags and create a three-sided wall of them around the crater lip, then goes to work with a small toolkit. Half an hour later the sandbag wall has four sides and a length of cord running to it from the ATO, stationed on a knee fifteen metres away. He wants a thirty-metre exclusion zone. He's about to blow it up. Excited, we all crane in to watch. He gives us a thirty second warning. Eagerly we countdown in our heads. At about minus five there is a small pop like a tiny balloon being burst. No flashes, no earth showering down. Just one small pop. Disappointed, we clear off back to lines and I ready my kit for vehicle patrol, making sure I have all my boxed ammunition in the top of my daysack and 100 rounds of loose link coiled by my side in my respirator pouch.

We patrol out as the morning stretches on. The brisk autumn winds whistle past the steel doors of main gate as we sweep past the Riflemen manning the bunkers. Two vehicles make our patrol and I in the lead turret. We rush out into the stony desert, where the camel herding nomads huddle around their fires.

The mist hangs in the wadi stubbornly, clinging on until the high-morning sun will force it to sigh away. My fingers are numb and the cold bites my face as we drive at speed through the desert dunes and up towards the main highway. We turn west, tracking the road but safely removed from it to thwart IEDs. Cars rush by, and we stop and watch and wait.

Finally, towards the end of the patrol, we find the launch site. Scorched and blackened earth marks where the rocket roared into life, and there are a few marks in the ground where the launch frame had been erected. We hang around for a while, marking the point on a map and reporting back over the radio. The Taliban are long since gone, this patch of desert is far from any compound and hidden from view from the main wadi.

We patrol back to Bastion, and I finally get some rest.

13. CATFORD

The WMIK roars like a caged beast freed, cloying grey dust billowing behind into zephyr-sighs as we speed across the plains. The red glint of dawn splashes new light across the shallow wadis and stone-pocked desert. The gentle warmth in the air hints at summers gone, fighting the passing year with a sad reluctance that is reflected in us all.

The first excitements of being in country have waned, the novelty replaced with weary routine. Night-time rocket attacks have shocked us into tense vigil as dusk sets in and the sand flies come to feed. When the attack sirens howl, adrenaline spikes into our pulse and we wake in an instant, hitting the floor, clawing our way into armour and helmets, and waiting to hear the impact.

This morning, after such a night, our vehicle patrol is tasked to cover the northern edge of the AO, whilst our sister patrol roams south at the edge of the wadi and Nad Ali. We are searching for the latest launch site with the Battalion Intelligence Officer, who will mark it on a map back at Bastion, to try and see where the Taliban will come from, and where they will launch from next.

We are free agents, roaring up and down the Pashtun lands, over hills and through valleys that are vaguely familiar from patrols past, and watching, always watching. My gun swings outwards, behind us, now brought to bear on a compound, now swinging outwards again, now watching back behind us as we weave and power away, churning up the ground. Andy and Vince sit in the front of my WMIK, leading the patrol. As well as hunting for the launch site, we are to show our presence to the villagers here, which means meandering between a few tiny villages, before making for Checkpoint Catford. Catford is sited on the road to Gereshk and manned by the ANP, the Afghan National Police.

My shemagh is tight across my mouth to keep the dust and cold at bay, my goggles are snapped down and I have planted my legs wide against the ammo racks to keep from being shaken loose from the GPMG turret. Our two-vehicle patrol made our way out of camp in the last hours of darkness, laagered up for dawn in all-round defence just shy of Highway One, and now we are loose and on task. The WMIK ride shakes me to my bones, Andy is enjoying himself at the wheel, and we are speeding across the plain, much faster than our usual patrol pace.

Our first village is only a mile or so away, and in only short minutes we are racing into position on the high ground just before the village. My WMIK takes overwatch position on the high ground, Vince covering the village with his passenger mount GPMG, and I complete the arc by watching across to Highway One. Pashtun farmers stop working with their hoes and picks, boys run around like pups at play, and within a few minutes the village headman is standing outside a compound, looking at us, watching us watch him. Griff's vehicle crawls downslope, and the village headman comes up. Jamshed is our interpreter, a small young man from a Tajik town somewhere in the north of Afghanistan. He is dispatched out of the Vector, and politics occurs. I eat a thrice-melted and re-set chocolate bar to pass the time, gun oil dripping from the GPMG and pooling on the metal floor beside my feet, whilst tactical radio chatter passes back and forth of who can see what.

'Highway One — empty,' I add to the mix when it's my turn, and attention passes back to the villagers.

Unconcerned minutes later, we set off in file and stop a few minutes past the village. Our vehicle swings in an arc and parks up beside the Vector, facing rearwards, so that the passenger side vehicle commanders can talk off the radio. I swing my turret around to face behind us, and listen in.

The first village don't like us being here. We offered them water, which they took without gratitude, and asked us when we are leaving.

Griff explained through Jamshed that we were leaving in a few minutes.

'No, when are all of you leaving? The Taliban are always here, asking us if we have seen you, asking us if we are helping you, asking us for money to help them fight you.'

Griff then asked them through Jamshed where the Taliban are, where do they come from, which way do they go? The villagers say the Taliban come and ask questions, and that was all the information they were willing to give.

◊ ◊ ◊ ◊ ◊

We make our way to the next village, a larger cluster of compounds and farms. Here there are pallid yellow melons growing in scrapes, fields covered in cut straw mulch, broken motorcycles propped against compound walls and a few tiny, bedraggled sheep roaming amongst the detritus, picking at the dead stems. Again I am tasked with watching the rear, and swing my turret around, lock off the traverse, and settle into as comfortable a position as I can manage.

The skies are darkening grey, with a westerly wind that stings my cheeks with every bitter gust, and the storm clouds are slowly gathering on the far horizon. Although I can't see the village from my position, when the wind drops I can smell the farmyard hints of livestock and slurry, fresh turned earth, and just a hint of woodsmoke.

The radio chatter continues, and the negotiations

continue behind me. A few cars speed along Highway One, but we are further north and as long as they don't stop or show an interest, they are of no concern to us.

◊ ◊ ◊ ◊ ◊

Vince laughs, and I turn to see what has happened. A sheep has wandered up to the WMIK, and a boy, tasked with shepherding duties, starts to run towards us to collect it. But then he gets closer, and stops, scared; caught between his duty to recover the sheep, and his fear of us. Vince takes his helmet off, smiles, and waves him over. Vince took an army course in Pashto, and has not had a chance to use his skills, so he is delighted for the chance. He calls out to the boy in Pashto, and the boy shouts something back, but stays a wary distance. Vince grabs a bottle of water from the WMIK floor and opens a packet of rations. He shouts something else, and again waves the boy to come. The boy pauses, thinks, then sidles closer to accept the gifts. He cannot be more than six or seven, a tiny, stick-figure thin waif in dirty tunic and Pashtun hat. He is barefoot, with matted black hair sticking out in all directions from under his hat. His dust-streaked face is marked with two runnels cleaned by fresh, glistening snot, and piercing blue eyes that never leave Vince, as he slowly steps close enough to snatch the food, then he jumps back. Vince keeps talking in Pashto, but the boy only replies a few brief words. The boy tucks the water bottle and food in his waistband, makes a grab for the sheep by the fleece, and drags it back towards the village, looking over his shoulder fearfully every few steps to make sure we haven't changed our minds about the gifts.

I call back to Vince, 'What did you say to him, then?' Vince doesn't answer. Perhaps he is embarrassed that his language skills are more rudimentary than he would have us believe. I try again, 'What did you give him?'

'Nothing much, just some crackers and cheese paste. And water.'

Chalky laughs. 'In Ireland there were gutter kids trying to get something from us. Food, kit, money, cigarettes, you name it. We'd break up a hexiblock into perfect square, shape it with a knife, then wrap it up real nice, y'know, so it looks good, then you'd eat a piece of Kendal mint cake. The kids would go nuts, begging, so you'd just open a pouch and give them the whole slab of hexi. Haa ha!'

We watch as the boy makes his way back to the rest of the villagers. A man, perhaps his father, marches up to the boy, snatches the water and food wrapper, and smacks him on the head, shouting at him. The boy runs inside the compound and is lost to sight. Then half a minute later, a procession of children are led out of the compound. They range from toddler size to young adult, and I count ten of them although they are jostling and moving. The father holding the water bottle looks at us, making the two fingers and thumb, waving hand gesture in front of his mouth that we recognise as a request for food. His children are lined up, patiently waiting.

Griff has had enough of this sideshow, and Jamshed is ordered back into the Vector, and we make ready to move, then the drivers drop the handbrake, open the throttle, and we kick up dust as we roll off. My wagon is the trail vehicle for now, and I watch back towards the village as the father stands motionless, watching us leave, and I wonder how the few crackers will be shared out once we have gone.

◊ ◊ ◊ ◊ ◊

We drive across a handful of shallow wadi beds, then up onto rocky dunes where the drivers gun the engines and power on eastwards towards Gereshk, handrailing Highway One. Griff calls over the radio and stops the patrol. New orders came from Zero, the radio operator at the command-and-control centre. We are to move to Catford to hand over supplies that the patrol has been carrying for days. We are close to an old Russian minefield marked with cathead cobbles, a splash of red paint on the mineward side.

We divert to avoid the mines and punch our way off the desert and onto Highway One. Here the WMIKs are free to speed down the centre of the road like a presidential convoy. We fire flares at any cars coming the other way, and they dive off and pull over until we have passed. If they ignore the flare, our next move would be to fire rounds of burning red tracer, first a warning shot, then through the windscreen aiming for the driver. Most cars pull off when they see us, and only the brave need the first warning flare to remind them.

We are closer to Gereshk than Nad Ali, at the eastern fringe of our AO and within sight of the farmsteads and compounds that are scattered around the outskirts of the town. We have not patrolled here as often as we have the central, western wadis, down south by Nad Ali or up north on the plains beyond Highway One. The firing points I am ranging are new, the villages only half-recognised, and each new car passing by flashes with faces at the windows, watching us in split seconds as Highway One draws them quickly past.

Exposed in my gun turret, the wind whips about me and cuts through my layers of cotton smock and woollen jumper, as the WMIK drivers push the vehicles as fast as they can go. Within a few short minutes we have arrived at Checkpoint Catford.

◇ ◇ ◇ ◇ ◇

Catford is manned by the ANP, as drug-addled and corrupt a bunch of police — if you can call them that — as you can imagine. In reality, they are bandits in uniform, who use check points as a way to extort the local population and line their pockets with bribes and protection money. If anyone were to ask, they are our allies and trusted partners in keeping Afghanistan safe from the Taliban. We stop short of their fortified base beside the highway and call them on the radio.

The ANP swarm out like wasps, draped with ill-fitted drab, grey uniforms, Kalashnikov rifles hanging from their necks or slung over their backs. Jamshed and Corporal Griff go out to meet the headman, and hand over supplies. Amidst the cacophony, I unlock the traverse on my gun turret and watch my arc, waiting for the order to patrol onwards, and away from here.

That night, I am on sangar duty, and the sky in the distance to the north east is illuminated orange. The ANP at Catford are firing parachute flares over and over. Each one blooms into life in the night sky over the plains, and slowly sinks until the light is quenched. We call the ops room to report there may be an attack in progress, but after a while it becomes clear that they are firing them off for fun. After the parachute flares are gone, they fire green and red hand flares, barely visible pinpricks of fleeting colour.

My sangar duty passes otherwise uneventfully, and I make my way back to company lines in the morning. That night at O-Group we hear that ANP Catford have complained that we didn't bring enough supplies, and they need more. Another platoon will be dispatched to resupply them, on another day.

14. BREAD

It is nearly five o'clock and the kettle in the gatehouse hisses to a crescendo. I remove the broken lid and top up a pair of Styrofoam cups, whisking then retrieving the teabag with a biro. We drink tea like the Afghans drink it: black with plenty of sugar, and too many times a day to count, as a hot sweet tea is almost as good as a meal. They have stopped feeding us, on gate sentry. The Irish Rangers used to drive out plates of hot food from the cookhouse, sangar to sangar to bunker to gatehouse, and every man had a bite. But the Irish are gone, and our daily rations consist of a few biscuits to share between all the men on sentry duty.

I am off duty after a day of sentry on main gate but am inexplicably filled with altruistic desire to make sure my comrades on the bunker are kept well supplied with hot tea. I sling Bella onto my back, and in full armour, start the walk through the Hesco lanes out to the gate, guardedly carrying the teas. It is a few minutes' walk, and I stride out until I see Cooper on the bunker, and a soldier from the Princess of Wales' own Royal Regiment. I step inside and hand Cooper a tea. We wait. A car comes, then another.

Bastion is an experiment in economics. It draws in locals to work in menial jobs, from building roads, working at the

71

burn pits, working in the water bottling plant, or working in the sewage plant. It pays them in crisp, fresh US dollars, which in turn find their way into the local economy. Some of those dollars will find their way into the pocket of the owner of the car I am waiting for. It is Thursday, and he is only ten minutes late, which is as good as punctual for a Pashtun. The familiar beaten-up white sedan crawls to a stop beside the bunker, with two men sitting up front. Cooper and I set to work as the PWRR soldier watches on. Salaams are exchanged, passes are checked and then the vehicle must be checked. The Pashtuns get out, the younger from behind the wheel, the elder from the passenger side.

Cooper takes charge from here. 'No, you can't come in.'
The old Pashtun looks uncomprehendingly.

'No. Pass, bad. No.' Cooper waves an arm back towards the desert. 'You,' he points, 'go.'

The younger Pashtun man claps his hands together like in prayer — please — but we are having none of it. They confer in their language, and the older man says a word then turns his back on us. He does not want to see what comes next. The younger reaches into the back seat through the window and lifts the cloth off a platter of bread, intended for the camp workers' supper. They are stacked high. Each piece is the size of a large pizza, and somewhere between lavash, the Iranian unleavened bread, and the more familiar naan bread. The younger man gives us a piece, not a bribe, heavens no. A gift. Cooper reconsiders and waves them through, completely unconnected to the fact he is holding a warm, fresh baked bread. He tears me off a quarter, and I munch slowly, savouring the delight of hot food.

'Those lazy bastards eat better than us,' he says through mouthfuls of fresh bread, and I turn and make my way back through the Hesco lanes to the gatehouse. My bread is eaten by the time I arrive, and I make my way off the front gate to arrive back at Wyvern Lines.

15. IRT – NIGHT

Darkness has come, and I find myself on my first IRT flight to pick up a casualty. From a standby tent, we were crashed out to the flight line, and I clambered aboard the helicopter and found my seat by feel. Now we have lifted and are racing away into the night. The emplaning ramp, half lowered, heaves like a window into the outside world. Dark and hunched like a vulture the rear gunner crouches over a machinegun pointing back over the flight line. We sit inside the Chinook in darkness, the double rotors screaming and battering my ears, vibrations shaking the air in my lungs. Two rows of infantry sit in lines against the rivets of the hull, staring blankly at one another in the dark as the helicopter contours the ground below. I check my machinegun again and tighten the strap that holds my ammunition to my belt. The exhaust heat pours back behind us distorting the air so that the whole world seems to be transformed by the terrific power of the engines.

Looking back at the night of the desert below, I see single lights of compounds dotting the ground like stars. So too the stars, turned orange by the heat haze and only the brightest visible, peek at us through the window of the lowered back-ramp, so that it is impossible to tell where the horizon is, which lights are stars and which lights on the ground. Amidst this cacophony of noise and dust-whipped flight, we sit, deaf and near-blind, alone with our thoughts.

Tight lips press down on grit teeth, brows furrow and eyes close. The overwhelming power of the Chinook, observed from inside its belly, is more intimidating than I had imagined. I look around again, trying to take my mind off the nagging feeling that our helicopter will be shot down by a Stinger missile, or crash and burn with us all inside. In the darkness of the flight, however, there is no refuge for the mind; the present always comes back with every shudder of the air currents, every turn or course adjustment the pilot makes. The desert slips by, on our way to Gereshk.

The desert quite suddenly gives way to a blanket of pin-prick lights marking the edges of a town. We must be flying over or into Gereshk, the night air over the compounds bright with lights. We bank and wheel and are about to land. As we lower down into a landing in a FOB in Gereshk I curse and fiddle with my seatbelt buckle, which is caught on my ammo pouch by my waist. I pull down my night vision monocle and flick it on as we bump down, and I free myself from my straps. The world becomes a dim green glow as the night vision shows me the softest light and brightens it. The smell of sand and petrol rush in and as we settle down on the second bump, I stand to jump off the ramp and bring the casualty in. The soldier to my left pulls me back into my seat and I hear a shout in my ear but can't make out the words over the din of the rotors roaring. I look around to see the infanteers standing on the canvas seats, and I follow suit. The reason becomes clear, as a gang of soldiers appears up the ramp, heaving a body on a canvas sheet. They surge and push past us in the cramped airframe, then lower the casualty to the floor. They make their way off the ramp, as we clamber down off the seats and sit again.

The helicopter lifts with a judder, and spins as it lifts, then the nose tips down and we power away through the night, invisible to the Pashtun eyes below. My eyes are drawn to the casualty as we rush him to the hospital. He is an Afghan soldier of the ANA, lying wounded on his back on a tarpaulin, his skinny frame crumpled, lying like a rag doll. In the dim green glow of my night vision, shadows flit across the helicopter medics, working on the man. Blood oozes through dressings on his chest, a thick dark green shade to my artificial night vision sight. I watch, heart racing, feeling sick and relieved at once that we are heading back to camp without a fight. At first, he lifts his arm to the sky, weakly grasping. Then his arm falls back to his side, fist working, clenching and unclenching slowly. He dies halfway back to Bastion.

We carry his broken corpse off on a new aluminium frame stretcher that we manoeuvre the dead weight of his body onto, and load it into an ambulance. The doors slam, and he is driven through the warm night to the bright electric comfort of Bastion hospital. We clamber back into the Chinook, and a quick lift takes us back to the flight line. We land, deplane, and a stripped-down Land Rover drives the infantry back to our tent, the IRT ready room. Sweat clings to the small of my back, cold and clammy, the excitement of the flight gone, replaced by weariness. We hop off the Land Rover, and I trail kit from my shoulders and arms as we drag our gear back inside the tent.

A debrief follows, where all mention of fear is excised with a surgeon's precision, and I recount the flight, the FOB landing, the casualty, and the outcome to the teams on standby. We sit on cotbeds under bright yellow light in the IRT tent, waiting for another call to the flight line, until the advancing night breaks our conversations into a dull murmur, and then the lights die and we lie awake until each man in his turn succumbs, and surrenders to sleep.

16 - PATROL – NORTH AND SOUTH

W e're patrolling the northern edge of our AO, across Highway One, closer to the mountains but still on the desert plains that lead from the foothills down into Nad Ali. Gently undulating dunes ripple across the landscape, hiding compounds and fields. It's sparse up here, unlike the newly-turned poppy fields away south on the outskirts of Nad Ali.

Our wagons roll on, Bazza's vehicle draws level with mine and I spin my gun turret to face outwards. Ahead of us, across grey stone and shingle lies a small wadi, the treacherous soft sand sown through with tell-tale tumbled pebbles. We cross warily in our vehicles, then with a roar of engines power up to the high ground on the other side. From here we can see the expanse of Dasht-e Margo laid out to the south, the sangars of Bastion just visible on the horizon, Bastion marked with a radio mast and a ghastly pallor of black smoke rising from the burn pits. Highway One is visible too, a kilometre or more south of us, with passing traffic glinting as cars race by.

The picturesque scene is my arc, and I clamber out of my turret, remove my helmet and sit, legs dangling, whilst we watch and wait. Chalky switches the radio on to BFBS, the British forces radio station, and we listen to the tinny strains of the latest pop songs. I shout across to Jacobs to watch my arc for a second, and climb into the back of my wagon, rummaging amongst the kit and ammunition boxes. I find some stowed rations, and pull out a tin of chicken pâté and hard biscuits. It's a relaxed situation for a patrol, and I climb back to my post, and munch away on my meal whilst I watch my arc again.

Lorries come and go along Highway One, several flights land in Bastion, and a pair of Chinooks lifts and flies east, accompanied by an Apache. Radio traffic is confined to the usual chatter: radio checks and location updates from our other patrol, who are patrolling the central wadi closer to Nad Ali. Bazza's voice comes through on the radio every twenty minutes or so, as he transmits from the other wagon, telling Zero that we still haven't moved. The radio airwaves crackle and distort our voices, and the radio traffic takes our thoughts and speech and voices away, high into the stratosphere, away from the desert and Afghanistan and the fighting, to bounce around the sky, fading and dying slowly over the years.

We are part of history, our patrol, one tiny flutter in a symphony that has no end. Years later, at home or in foreign lands, we walk under the shroud of radio traffic through grey streets and towns and lives, beneath unheard voices, years old, obsolete in the upper atmosphere, telling our former location in our former lives to no-one.

◊ ◊ ◊ ◊ ◊

We hold the ground in an overwatch position for an hour or so, until the sun has flooded the western sky orange, and visibility begins to close in from the horizon. Our patrol is scheduled to stay out until 0300 though, so whilst the dimming day heralds an end to work for some, we still have ground to cover, work to be done whilst our troops in Bastion sleep through the night.

We move off after dusk, headlights blazing, sights raised, guns up, bodies low, a unit moving together in harmony but each man alone with his thoughts hanging over him. The highway buzzes under rubber as we push towards the white and orange lights of Camp Bastion. As we make our way onto the dune-flanked capillary road, we go dark, both vehicles kill the lights. Drivers switch to their night sight, and they drive with soft green light to their faces and take us off road, circling back. We sweep around to set up a snap ambush on the road. I face rear to the west and for a quarter of an hour we sit, silent, watching and waiting.

Like every day and every night before in this country, we watch and wait. No clock can count just how the hours age you, as the wind pricks around your frame, cold shudders through you, and your numb fingers flex to try in vain to find some warmth in your bones. This night, we wait and watch in snap ambush order before we move north again. Eyes on Highway One, armoured wagons holding armoured bodies, our thoughts and dreams are wrapped in layers of loneliness as each man wrestles fatigue.

Tonight, we are patrolling with the intent to catch the mortar team that has been firing on FOB Juno or the Taliban unit that has been firing 107mm rockets into camp. Often we patrol with headlights on full beam, advertising the presence of our two vehicles. I think that this is madness, that by showing everyone where we are, and also how few of us there are, we are asking for trouble; that one of these days we will drive into a night ambush, and the first rounds incoming will light up the night with a crackle of muzzle flashes.

I prefer to go out on night patrols with Bazza instead of Griff, who patrols in one direction for a few minutes with headlights on, then goes black — switches to IR headlights or simply uses the light of the moon — and swings us around in a loop, to sit and wait set back from the path we just drove to see if anyone is following us, as we have just done. Sometimes we patrol using only black light, and sometimes we patrol with headlights on, one behind the other but separated by a hundred metres, so that anyone watching would think that we are the front and back vehicles of a much larger patrol.

◊ ◊ ◊ ◊ ◊

I had always thought of deserts as sandy, barren, and as flat as pancakes; with nothing stretching to every horizon, nowhere to hide, and nothing to see. The desert here, however, is a more complicated affair. The wadi floor, as vast as a glacial valley, a kilometre wide at the narrowest, is dirt and sandy earth. But the majority of our AO is made of the stony, rolling mega-dunes that rise up from the valley floor on each side, criss-crossed with spurs and re-entrants, mini-valleys that join the main wadi, sunken and hidden plateaus, a rugged landscape as complicated as it is dangerous. The risk of a vehicle getting bogged down in soft sand is ever-present, and after the rains the farmers' fields are quagmires to suck us into a wheel-spinning panic. The closer to Nad Ali we are, the more dangerous it is.

◊ ◊ ◊ ◊ ◊

One October morning we are patrolling in two vehicles with the boss leading us. He takes us south. We skirt Bastion's south edge, driving through the re-entrant that the camp sewage drains into, known as sewage river. A small village has sprung up here. In 2012 this will be the launching point for a suicide attack on Bastion that destroys six Harriers and kills two US marines. Now, it consists of some empty compounds and a few fields; freshly harvested and prepared to winter over with the stems of dead poppy strew over the dirt.

We drive through sewage river village and join the main wadi minutes later, heading towards Nad Ali and the edge of our AO. I am wrapped up against the cold, goggles down, bouncing around on top cover with my GPMG cocked. The boss doesn't like us riding with cocked weapons, but I am confident with my muzzle drills so always cock surreptitiously after we leave camp, as it would be faster to flick off the safety and fire than it would be to cock the weapon and fire. We roar through the wadi, powering to the top of the dunes on the far side, and make our way south east, ever further away from Bastion and ever closer to the edge of our AO.

After maybe half an hour, the scattered compounds become ever denser. Odd trees and bushes dot the landscape, and the more there are, the more wary I get. We are driving into thickly populated areas, more people are visible in the fields around us, turning to stare as we pass by. We stop on the downslope of a hill and see Nad Ali spread about before us. There are walls and dykes, treelines demarking property, well-driven roads marked in the dirt. My whole body is tense. For the last half hour, I have been ranging compounds in my head, so that if there is a contact I won't have to think about ranges, I will automatically know the distance to the firing point. In the wadi my range slider on the backsight of the GPMG was set to eight hundred metres, as the compounds opened up away from us. As we moved south the compounds pressed in closer and closer to our patrol.

Now we have entered Nad Ali outskirts, and my range slider is set to two hundred metres. I can see the canal ahead of us, rows of trees growing on the banks either side. I feel sick with worry, as it would take a miracle for us to come through a contact unscathed. One vehicle down, and we would have only one means of escape. Two vehicles lost, and we are all as good as dead. We could never hope to fight our way on foot all the way back through the villages, only six of us, and it would take at least twenty minutes for Cobra air support to get here, assuming our radios get in touch with base, which sometimes they can't do even when we can see the antennae of Bastion. I have only 1,000 rounds of 7.62mm and 800 of 5.56mm, which might just last until the Cobras came.

The boss stands up in the front of the WMIK and surveys Nad Ali with binoculars. We turn back for Bastion, pushing towards the main wadi. In the rear vehicle, facing back towards Nad Ali I see dust churning behind us as we race away, until we reach the sparse, flat dune tops of the high ground on the east of the central wadi.

We make our way back to Bastion slowly, stopping on high ground to overwatch the traffic in the wadi. We relax, helmets off, radio on, alternating watch. One top cover takes the rear whilst the other stands down, the driver or vehicle commander watching the ground ahead. I sit on the frame of the WMIK, legs dangling, helmet off and shemagh around my head, eating cold rations that seem to be left over from the 80s. My cares of a few hours ago of the southern border seem as far away as the life I left behind at home, and for a while, things seem almost normal. We could be anywhere in the world, underneath the sun, eating and smoking and laughing together — except for the constant watch, and the constant threat at the back of our minds. We finish our watch, and patrol back to camp, handover to the outgoing patrol, and another day is done.

17. COMING OFF MAIN GATE

The sun's fading fire had finally quenched somewhere in the western desert, the burnt orange giving way to a thousand darkening shades of rich blue and silent, deep purple. Stars were springing up in the east, and a peaceful stillness settled over the entranceway to Bastion. As the night shrouded us, so too the activity of another day tailed off, leaving Cooper and I in a bunker on the road out of camp. We relish the silence, relaxing away the last few minutes of our day's sentry duty. The gate has already been closed for the night, and I am content just to sit and gaze out into the desert.

Somewhere out there, in the vast desert plains of AO Robin, the conflict continues between ISAF and Taliban, but it is far beyond our sight and understanding. The AO is nearly one thousand square kilometres, and I can see a scant few hundred metres out into the desert. Beyond that point, the deeds of night are unseen and unknown.

Cooper taps his fingers impatiently, and the noise is followed by the snap of a tobacco tin, he rolls a cigarette, and I stare out into the night beyond us — and the cool night air is split open by an explosion close by our bunker, maybe a hundred metres to the south. It is like a clap of thunder that reaches out and punches us in the chest, and Cooper and I look at each other like rabbits, eyes wide and hackles raised. Then I grab my helmet and dive onto the floor just as a spluttering hiss whines through the air above our heads, and another thunderclap sounds away in the camp to the north. Cooper clips his helmet to his head and sits in the corner of the bunker. Away to my left in the Danish lines, rises a noise — shouting, boots on stone, doors slamming. My heart is racing, and every second I expect more rockets to land around us, showering the bunker with white-hot fragments of supersonic metal like a shotgun blast, and mixed with an acid fear is incredulity. Someone wants to kill me, I think, and I can hardly believe it.

Despite watching the ANA warrior dying on the IRT flight, the violence of war still seemed far away from us in Bastion, and now it has come to find us. Ten seconds pass, then another.

'Last round?' I venture to Cooper, who looks unsure.

'Must be,' he says, and we call in on the HF radio to the Ops room to report the attack.

The attack came just as shifts were changing over, our relief from 1 Platoon were already marching out to our bunker, and just like that, the rocket attack was over, and I am stood down to return to company lines. I trudge my way back to my tent, helmet on and wary of more rounds landing, watching around me for cover, in drainage ditches, beside Hesco walls. Adrenaline gone, I feel a growing anger — at the Taliban who have attacked us, at my unit commanders for keeping us back in camp instead of hunting and killing our attackers — and I tell myself that we will catch this Taliban rocket team sooner or later. There is no more attack for now, and I reach lines uneventfully.

The tent is nearly empty, most men are out patrolling, on sangar duty, or on IRT, and those who are here are sleeping sound. No attack alarm sounded, and when morning comes they will hear of the rockets. For now, I do my best to join them in sleep, but adrenaline is pumping through me and I lie awake for hours before I finally rest.

18. STAG

The bastard!' I am raging. 'What an absolutely useless bastard.'

Jacobs sits to my left, like me his back against the Hesco barrier at the front gate complex, listening to my rant.

'It's so simple, and he screws it up. Every bloody time.' I slam a magazine home into Bella's magazine housing, loading my weapon in preparation for a night on front gate sentry duty. 'Two sangars, one bunker, and he turns the stag list into a carousel!'

Jacobs, unfazed, tweaks and teases a wad of tobacco onto a cigarette paper. We are on our arses down in the dust, twilight advancing, about to march through the command centre to the forward bunker and forward sangar. Bastion has a recessed entranceway, so in order to reach the main gate you have to make your way through a complex weaving road, constrained by ditches, passing by the gaze of sangars and bunkers until you reach the entrance gate proper. The rear sangar overlooks the whole entrance, the front sangar watches vehicles from the time they round the corner of the dusty road to Highway One, and the final position is the front bunker — the rotten apple in the batch — where Cooper and I were a few nights ago when rockets were

85

flying over us. The front bunker holds a pair of soldiers, one of whom will leave to stop any vehicle and check their pass, playing Russian roulette with his life in the hope that there are no suicide bombers.

Mosquitoes whine around our heads, looking for the soft neck skin to their evening feed. They are late to the party. Sandflies, tiny black pin pricks, cluster where they can find blood, at the wrist and forearm. We brush them away, scraping them off with the back of a knife, but within minutes there will be more to take their place. Luckily, they only feed at dusk, so within an hour there will only be raised red welts as a reminder. I slap my neck suddenly, hearing (or did I imagine it?) a mosquito close by my right ear, but I miss.

Jacobs allows me to continue, 'What he should do, is stick two of us in each sangar, close them up for the night, lock them in, and have the three Tiger boys rotate bunker, sucks to be them.'

Jacobs nods his agreement, pursing his lips as he starts the delicate process of folding the cigarette paper back on itself.

Because we have men out at FOB Keenan and FOB Edinburgh, three lads from PWRR- The Princess of Wales's own Royal Regiment, known as 'The Tigers', have been sent to help us fill our duties. The stag list that the target of my ire Corporal Ozzy has drawn up sees each man undertaking an hour in each position, then all moving to the next position instead of treating the sangars as self-contained positions to be manned by two men. Leaving sangars single-handed means that the cages are left open, not locked for the night, and all the men on rest share a crowded room full of cots, with no chance for sleep as every so often someone will get to their feet, noisily haul the weapon and kit up, to trudge out to front bunker. My stag list, where Jacobs and I get a sangar to ourselves to watch through the night is infinitely preferable — more so if it's rear sangar, which we volunteered ourselves for earlier in the day to Corporal

Ozzy.

'Awwh fellas, I'll let you know where you'll go,' he said, but we were sure we would have an easy night of it.

I continue my rant to Jacobs, 'How simple. But no, he thought, "How can I mess Addy and Jacobs about the most." You think a PWRR Corporal would look after his boys? Course he would. He'd sort them out with a sangar. But this colonial idiot has to make it so that no-one gets any sleep at all.'

Jacobs licks the cigarette paper, and with a final roll, seals it up. Without a word, he holds it in front of my face. I take it between my lips, close my eyes and suck as a match flame is proffered. I smack my lips, acrid and bitter, blow out the first smoke and put the cigarette back between my lips to draw in a breath of the soothing haze. I exhale a thin cloud, and instantly I feel better. I take another drag, head lolling back against the Hesco, feeling the anger subside and my head is suddenly clear.

'Thanks, I needed that.'

Jacobs takes the cigarette from my hand and lights his own from the glowing red tip. 'Ready then mate?'

I am ready. We heave to our feet, cradle our weapons, and with cigarettes tucked in the corner of our mouths, we trudge out towards front bunker and the start of a sleepless night.

19. COMING OFF PATROL ONTO IRT

Weighed down by armour, I lift my kit and weapon onto my shoulders. Silence surrounds me but for the gentle crunch of my boots shifting sand, and in the gloaming I make my way from the front gate sangar back to Wyvern lines. We follow the dirt-packed road that snakes around the perimeter of the camp, and the ditches either side for the rains that will fall later this year. Every so often a Land Rover or armoured vehicle rushes by, blinding me with the headlights' glare, so that I stop still until they have passed to keep myself from straying into the ditch, or into their path. I stop-start my way to the company HQ as night approaches.

The tart, warm smell of dirty clothes, oil and sweat rises up to greet me as I shoulder my way through the door to my tent. My kit slaps down beside my bed, boots hurriedly taken off, then I lie down on my cot and close my eyes, exhaling my cares away with a deep, rich satisfaction. I stretch out, ignoring everything but the feeling of cool air over my bare toes, then I place the soles of my feet on the cold fabric of my sleeping bag, worming my toes deep into the material and feeling the heat wick out of them. I have a few hours of down-time before I must report to the IRT tent, and I plan on enjoying them as best I can. I might even have a letter from Charlotte waiting in the CQM offices and relish the prospect of mail.

Vince arrives at the tent as I am cooling my feet down, and I look up to see him pass by the entranceway to my admin area. He is puffed and red-faced from the chill, hauling his gear as I did across one shoulder. We exchange quiet salutations, then I swing my legs off the cot-bed and reach for a stack of old letters. I don't want to check just yet if I have a new letter in case I don't. I savour the possibility as long as I can, and will resolve this uncertainty either with joy or disappointment in a short while. I settle back on my cot-bed, take an old letter from Charlotte and read.

The memory of my old life weights heavy on me too, except unlike my armour it is never truly taken off, nor is it too heavy that I can't forget it for a while, until a reminder stirs me. My road to Helmand started years earlier, in Plymouth. Graduating from university, I headed out into the world with my new degree, my excitement fading and jading me with each pay packet, as I worked an array of jobs, eventually settling for a job in insurance sales. Now that I was a common workaday nine–to–five administrator, my then- girlfriend left me to pursue big dreams in the music industry. I was despondent — at a loss, hurting and unsure of myself from our break-up, I resolved to find meaning through the eyes of external, imagined admirers.

So it was that I decided to become a soldier. Fondly basking in the awe and respect commanded by the sight of a false vision of myself, standing tall in uniform, a leaner, magazine-ready reimagining of the lost boy I found myself on the edge of the Tamar and the world, as the bombs fell and the bullets flew in Helmand.

I took The Queen's shilling in 2007, on the day before Halloween, and although the British Army no longer pays a day's wages for your oath, I can attest that I drank a day's wages of beer courtesy of my new platoon. I woke the next day naked on a new comrade's sofa and walked home wearing bin bags. So began my journey with the Army Reserves.

I passed out from the Combat Infantryman Course at Catterick in April, celebrated with more beer, and woke up naked. The next day, rumours of a deployment for my Rifle Regiment were fresh on the breeze. A nod and a wink to Serjeant Chris let him know that I was 'in', and papers arrived within the week, with an efficiency the army had scarce of in supply.

It feels like the life of another person, so completely unlike the reality of my life now, so much so that I can barely believe I had a life before the British Army. Lost in thought, I lie on my cot-bed filled with weariness, scarce able to move, haul myself to the cookhouse to eat and drink, or even bring myself to cross the walkway outside my tent to the wash block. Ten minutes or so pass, and the low chatter of voices outside Flint's tent dies down as men half-march to supper, emptying Wyvern Lines but for the few souls like myself. I sigh and swing my legs over the cot bed to the floor, finally ready to visit the wash block and wipe away the sweat, grime and dust.

◊ ◊ ◊ ◊

The next day I am on IRT, but the day passes slowly. There is one shout, a routine evacuation. The Chinook fleet is precious, so non-urgent evacuation is handled by a Sea King. There is only room for one infantryman on the Sea King flights, and today it was Vince's turn. After he has reported to the flight line, and we have waited enough time, he returns throwing open the entrance flap to the tent, and the wide grin on his face invites us all to ask.

They were high in the sky above the plains, circling, clearing the airspace as a fast air asset engaged a Taliban position. Vince saw it all through the porthole.

It was an A10 bombing run, dropping white phosphorus to 'mark the target''. Phosphorous is against the Geneva convention as a weapon, but it is allowed to use the smoke to mark targets. A fast air controller somewhere in Garmsir decided to play an Afghan game of Catch-22, marking a target that friendly troops 'couldn't see' so well that once they had seen it, they didn't need to see it because the target no longer existed. We drink tea whilst Vince tells us of the explosion, the fire, the thick smoke, and the terrifying beauty of the A10 swooping through the sky on the way to deliver death. We are a carousel of cruelty and compassion — gifts of water and food, salaam alaykum and respecting the Afghan culture, and burning men alive in their fighting positions. My duty passes uneventfully though, and before long I am due for sangar sentry, and then patrols after that. The carousel spins me around, and the world turns with us.

20. KHINEY

Khiney is the new craze in our unit, and we spend all our spare dollars on tins of it. Khiney is the stuff of locals, a modern snuff, a spiced and flavoured thumbnail-sized packet that is laced with nicotine. It is imported from Pakistan to the local bazaars and costs several dollars a tin. One packet on the gums gives a pleasant flavour like lime cordial, and a strong nicotine kick. It also makes the mouth water and makes us spit frequently.

We dip into tins before patrol to get a buzz before we head out. We take a fresh packet for the other cheek when our gums have gone numb on one side, but we still want more. Too much makes you feel sick though, so the biggest khiney-fiends find a balance between taking dips into their tin and not overdoing it. We take a quick dip before breakfast, to wake us up. We take slow and steady dips throughout the long, stretched out days on sangar watch. We take a dip after IRT to relax, and one after supper for something to do in the evenings. I become hooked on the stuff, taking a dip and spitting lime, savouring the flavour and the buzz, then discarding the packet quickly.

Like all crazes, our love affair with khiney burns out and is gone just as fast as it came, replaced by cigarettes. Straight rolled cigarettes were the mark of a green soldier when we first arrived, to be avoided at all costs in favour of hand-rolled tobacco. Now, all hooked on nicotine from our khiney addiction, we become connoisseurs of Afghan cigarettes, buying packets from the locals at whatever outrageous prices they can extort us for. I spend my time between patrols smoking with Jacobs, and we share cigarettes and light each other's in turn, keeping a mental tally of whose turn it is to give the other a straight or a roll up. With armoured backs against the Hesco, helmets resting by our sides and a cigarette drooping from my mouth, cheeks brushed with sand from the latest patrol, I imagine the picture we must paint- a snapshot of Afghanistan and Herrick 9. There is no-one to take our picture though. No-one to document, to freeze in time the magazine-ready soldier I imagine I have finally become. We smoke and patrol the days and nights away, and khiney is forgotten.

21. OPERATION BABENJI

Ablue-hazed dawn is threatening the reaches of night across the sky. The first touches of winter have taken root in the small hours, and the bleary-eyed sentries, alone in their sangars are blowing off their numb fingers and huddling into their own warmth. The vast expanse of dunes and wadis is silent and still, far beyond the gaze of the weary soldier on lookout. The mountains of the north and barren poppy fields of the south await the day, and from a lead-heavy sleep that weighs me down into my cot, I am roused by a rough hand shaking my shoulder in the dark. Red torchlights dance on the tent walls, as softly, with rustle and creak, our patrol rises and gathers our gear.

We stagger and trickle our way to the low Hesco barrier where Wyvern Lines opens onto the internal link road. I blink and rub my eyes, trying to clear my groggy head. Jacobs and Fisk plonk their daysacks down on the Hesco and share a roll-up whilst the rest of us in turn don our body armour, tighten straps, close and lock pouches, each man checking another. My helmet hangs on a carabiner on my chest, giving me a spare hand to close Vince's magazine pouch as he is checking Conlay's belt kit. A low background chatter punctuates our pre-patrol checks, murmurs and whispers until we are ready. As each man finishes his checks he shuffles back until we stand in a loose circle arranged around the back of our Vector waiting for the boss. We are in patrol order, daysacks and belt kit, ammo and water. We'll be patrolling on foot today.

The boss arrives, hurrying from the ops tent back to lines. He passes us on the way through the Hesco gate, and nods approvingly. 'Looking ally, men.' He disappears into the officers' tent to grab his gear. He lumbers over with his kit, dons his helmet, balances his rifle across his boots to sling a radio onto his shoulders, then stands cradling his weapon. 'Listen up men. You received patrol orders at the O-Group last night so this is just a quick reminder. Watch your arcs, do your 5 and 20s. Granite 50 call sign will escort us out, the engineers will let us know where they want to go, we protect them and sweep for IEDs. That's it. Radio checks and let's move.'

Vince and I jump in the back of the nearest Vector, Jacobs and Fisk in the other, Litch climbs into ours. Griff hauls himself in the commander's seat in the front and slams the armoured door shut. We keep the twin back doors open as long as possible, staring out at the tents of Wyvern Lines lit up by walkway lights, dawn now easing along and showing the gloomy arena of our tents and Hesco in pre-morning light. After a few minutes more of semi-rest, a vehicle patrol arrives to escort us out of camp, and we move off.

We bump and roll around in the back of the Vector as we head out of camp onto the road to FOB Tombstone. Winter is on the way, and the morning light creeping ever-on shows not the clearer skies that welcomed us to the country in azure splendour, but ominous, grey clouds that cover the sky to every horizon and dim the day. We approach our jumping-off point on the plains to the north, beside Highway One, a kilometre or two from camp. The Vector, WMIK and Snatch stop in column and top covers spin their turrets or swing gun mounts about to offer all-round protection.

Our patrol stumbles out in dribs and drabs, assembling down on one knee, waiting. The vehicle escort rolls off and heads back to camp, and our ten-man patrol is left alone in the desert. As they depart, a V of birds flies overhead, south to north, more harbingers of the changing seasons.

I survey my arc, ready to move off, seeing the landscape stretch out ahead of me, a muddy ochre with bland grey overhead. We are on the stony desert plains, the two engineer-surveyors are talking to the boss at the front of our section, appropriately surveying several maps at once and gesticulating at the ground ahead of us. Still down on one knee, between Bruce Lee and Litch, I wait patiently, as fifty kilos of weight presses down my kneecap into the stony ground. I am wearing a kneepad to ward off infanteers' knee, but the sheer weight I am carrying means that a dull pain is radiating through my leg as we wait to move off. Bruce Lee is also uncomfortable, as he shifts several times, twisting and leaning with a noisy rattle of kit.

'Didn't you soundproof your kit mate?' asks Litch, 'You sound like a skeleton wanking into a biscuit tin.'

I cannot help but laugh, but our fun is quickly ended. 'Keep it down men, you're not on exercise now, this is the real thing,' the boss calls to us.

I survey my arc as the first drops of the winter rains start to fall around us, splashing into the dust and dirt. Within minutes it is raining steadily, water pooling in the creases of my smock and running in rivers down my trousers, easing its way into my boots and drowning my mood as, cold and wet, we finally stand with a creak and shake out into file to begin our patrol.

We move about a kilometre, with good visibility all around, and the surveyors stop every so often with a ranging pole and take measurements. Then, we swing back towards camp and just as we are about to step off again after the boss has a word with the engineers, Bruce Lee collapses, calling out that his knee has given way and he can't walk. We stop, water vapour rising from our smock sleeves, our warmth from the exertion dispersing into the cold season. Bruce Lee is relieved of his kit and his daysack and extra ammunition are distributed amongst the patrol. I get the short straw and have the blue EWD, a relic of Northern Ireland days, at least twenty kilos if it's an ounce, a whirring electronic beast. I am helped to my feet after taking a knee to shrug the pack on.

I am weighed down like I have never felt before. My kit, weighed before I left, was fifty kilos including armour, helmet, weapon, ammo and water, and is now weighed down with machine gun ammunition and the EWD. With every step, pain shoots through my knees and my teeth clench in sympathy for the compression in my joints. Within minutes, I am leaning forwards with every step, to try and shift the load above my spine instead of pulling me backwards. Fighting would be impossible, it's all I can do to move myself forwards at a slow walking pace.

Step by grim step, the RV point comes closer, where we will call for vehicle pick-up and wait for a ride back to camp. Like a marathon runner who has hit the second wall and is running on empty, I set small goals for myself — just another ten steps, count them down. Then just another ten after that. In the longest minutes, where the mind forces the body to perform beyond its normal capacity, I feel that I can scarcely hold myself on my feet but somehow I manage to keep moving. I sigh with relief when the boss holds up a hand to stop the patrol, and we fan out into all-round defence. The unlucky three, myself among them, shrug the EWD off, and they stand on their ends in the middle of the RV point. I feel light-headed and about to float, although I still have the weight of my own equipment hanging off me. The radio crackles, and as I look down my gunsight, I hear the dull hum of far-off vehicles gradually rise until the escort vehicles are upon us. We load up, sitting awkwardly, crammed in amongst the patrol kit and daysacks at all angles. The rumble of the engines lets us know we are heading back to camp, and the top cover from 1 Platoon chews gum, leaning bored against the hatch, covering our rear whilst the juddering wheels hiss fresh mud into a thin spray behind us.

22. REST AND RECUPERATION

I have no calendar to count down the days, but soon enough we are two months into the deployment, and it's time for my R&R. I am not yet bone-weary of this place, but home I must go, so I pack up a bag, and stow my weapon, ammunition, armour and morphine in a shipping container locked by the company quartermaster. I head to the flight line to wait a Hercules flight to Kandahar. We board, and I strap in between cargo nets and canvas-covered air freight.

There are four infantrymen with me: my comrades from the Rifle Regiment who are being sent home too, and we are joined by a pair of Special Forces troopers on the flight. It is black when we take off and it's too noisy to talk over the din of the aircraft. Whilst the Hercules is thrown about in a steep climb, I close my eyes and try to picture home and what I'll do when I get there. I don't really know, except sleep for as long as I can. We arrive at Kandahar without incident, though during the descent the pilot hard targets us in so much that it feels like we are riding an out-of-control bucking bronco. The mood on the plane lightens when we land safely; Stingers and RPGs are a threat out here due to the dense urban sprawl to hide a firing point.

We stand around waiting by the edge of the runway before we are herded into a large tent to stand and wait some more. A gaunt-looking RAF officer addresses us, telling us to keep our armour with us at all times and showing us maps of the IDF shelters. After a long wait in this tent a single decker coach arrives to take us to our accommodation, and we arrive at a hangar filled with cot beds, row up on row, open to the air at both ends, perhaps the same we slept in on our way through to Helmand when we were arriving. From the moonlight spilling in we find our way to a cot, dump our kit, and after a wash and scrub of teeth I am ready to sleep. Travelling light, none of us have sleeping bags. I put a coat on and try to wrap up, knitting my shemagh about my head like a local and sticking my hands under my armpits. My thin desert trousers offer no warmth at all, and I take out my towel and spare shirt and drape them over my legs, trying to stay warm in the chill of the night. I get no sleep at all and shiver my way through to dawn.

Finally, the morning light goads my companions into rising, and we get up as a group to shower and shave. Ignoring advice about IDF, we stow our armour under our cot beds and make our way to the boardwalk and PX shops. The PXs are first on the way, and we stroll into the American PX and check out the wares. There are more protein powders and bodybuilding supplements here than in any shop back home. There are a variety of OEF t-shirts, army brown ones with 'infidel' in Arabic written on the chest, ones with flames and stars and stripes and cobras and cross hairs. I buy two pairs of desert socks, thick cotton with fast wicking loops and thin vent strips. They will wear through within a month, giving me blisters and I will go back to wearing the thick woollen British Army socks. Next, we head to the Dutch PX, which is a smaller shop but stocked with sensible luxury items: multi tools, beef jerky, waterproof rucksack liners, and baseball caps in desert cam.

We walk further towards the centre of camp and find the boardwalk. The boardwalk is just that, a huge triangular footway of planks raised about a foot above the ground, with room on each side for a shipping container converted into a shop. Containers are dotted all around the three sides, and we saunter about, looking to kill some time somewhere.

We follow our noses and find ourselves at the Subway. That settles it, breakfast today is Subway. First in the queue, I order a meatball footlong and have all but finished it before the last man has collected his order and taken a seat with us on the wooden chairs. Next are shops for souvenirs, clothes shops, phone card shops. We come to a closed red shipping container with an old oriental woman sitting outside it reading a book. She looks up when we stop.

Chalky approaches her. 'Morning, what's this here then?'

'Massage,' she snaps, looking unhappy at being disturbed.

We are not sure, we hang back, but then the door opens and a pretty young Asian girl sticks her head out and says something to the old lady, and as they chatter back and forth and our pretty Asian goes back inside, our minds are made up.

Chalky asks the question we are all thinking, 'How many beds are inside?'

The Asian lady smiles now that we are customers. 'Four girls, four massage tables. One hundred twenty dollar.'

'Each?' Chalky is shocked.

'Ooh yah!' She laughs like this is the funniest thing the old lady has ever heard. 'Thirty dollar each.'

Chalky and Bruce Lee check their wallets, and go inside. Peterson opens his wallet and groans. He has no money with him.

'Can I borrow some mate?' he asks. I have nearly one hundred dollars on me, so I hand over thirty dollars and Peterson goes inside. The Asian lady looks at me.

'You? Massage?' she asks.

I am not sure. My feet are in a bad way, I have been doing back-to-back vehicle patrols to cover the other multiple who had men on R&R, and keeping my boots on for so long in dirty socks has given me terrible athlete's foot. I am ashamed to show my filthy, red, crusty toes to a pretty young Asian girl. I shake my head. Her smile disappears and she ignores me.

I wander about to kill time, waiting for my comrades. Eventually the other Riflemen arrive out of the red shipping container. Two of them are beaming but Peterson's face tells a less happy story.

'What happened?' I ask. Peterson tells me how he stripped down to his boxers, athlete's foot and all, and the most beautiful Asian he had ever seen oiled him down and started to massage him. She worked up and down, unknotting muscles and unwinding stress. Once his back was finished he was turned over, and she massaged the front of his legs. She said that she liked him very much, that he was a good-looking boy. I crane closer to hear the story unwind. Peterson continues.

'She said how poor she was, how long it had been since she had chocolate, and was I going to give her extra money so she could buy chocolate for herself.' Peterson's face cracked and he sighed. 'You only gave me thirty dollars, I paid when I went in! I told her I had no more money, and she finished massaging me and gave me my clothes back!'

I laugh. 'You couldn't get laid in a whorehouse?'

He shakes his head sadly.

◊ ◊ ◊ ◊ ◊

After we land in Brize Norton the next morning, our spirits are high and every bad joke we tell raises guffaws and smiles as we wait in a queue in the main terminal for our rail warrants. The air is cool, the light streaming in through the glass sides of the building is reassuringly drab, and we are nearly able to turn for home — but first, we must get to

Oxford train station.

'Two buses per day, 1000 and 1600,' explains the warrant officer in charge of transport. 'Take these and board at the bus stop outside Gateway House.' He hands us sheets of white paper with 'Bus Pass' and the MOD logo printed on them. I try to ask him if there is any other way except the bus, but he is already explaining to the troops in the queue behind us that they have to take their bus passes and board at the bus stop outside Gateway House. It is just past 1030. The prospect of missing a day of R&R to sit around Brize Norton is so far removed from my idea of a good time, that I am at once deflated by the thought.

Luckily, Peterson has a plan. Instead of a rail warrant, he arranged a hire car through our Admin Officer before he left Kandahar. Since some troops had died recently by driving tired after a long journey home, the new rules said that you had to stay overnight in Gateway House and collect your car the morning after you arrive. Peterson though, simply changes his shirt in the toilets to a crisp, fresh pressed desert camouflage with no rank slide, and gives us his bags to carry. Then, he beckons us to follow him. We move over to the car hire desk. Peterson greets the desk clerk with a smile, and asks can he have his car now please? The clerk explains the rules regarding car hire. Peterson looks slightly confused.

'Yes, I know, I flew in yesterday. I've been waiting for my men.' He gestures at the rabble behind him.

Five minutes later we are packed into the back of a Vauxhall Astra, driving hell-for-leather for Oxford station. My deflated spirits soar, and I smile and laugh at every bad joke as we make our way to the station.

The reunion at Salisbury train station is a strange affair, a mixture of awkward embraces, tears from my mother, and I am pleased when my parents finally see me to the car. I feel like a child again, sitting in the back seat, looking at the traffic pass and the English countryside slide by as my father drives us along country lanes and carriageways. I feel sad, so very sad to be back, I was only just getting used to the country, and the army takes me away, teases me with what I can't have before throwing me back into the foothills of the Hindu Kush all over again.

It is mid-November. The trees are nearly bare, the orange glow of autumn has long been trampled underfoot in a slow mix of mud and weary footsteps. The crisp, clear days are drawing down into a cold winter, and already Christmas is in the breeze. Each day races by horribly. Each evening we sit in front of the television and I dread the next day, and how fast each one so far has gone. Each morning I sleep in and waste more of the day, but never feel fully rested.

◊ ◊ ◊ ◊ ◊

I head west a few days later, to visit the Bloody Eleventh platoon, and Charlotte. The train screeches its way to Plymouth, metal grating on metal whilst the countryside whips by.

The first night, I insist on taking us to the platoon bar. I surround myself with familiar faces, familiar jokes and jargon, whilst familiar beer sits heavier and heavier on my stomach and the hours march on. We are the guests of honour, new recruits coming and going, shaking me by one hand and pushing another glass into my other.

Charlotte doesn't ask questions like the rest of them do, but she is by my side as I dance over the deployment so far. I regurgitate lessons, politics and tactics, and they solemnly nod whilst I move units around for ISAF and rewrite policy, solving Afghanistan's problems between mouthfuls of lager.

Eventually the older soldiers have left for their beds, and the younger ones left for an after-hours dance club. Charlotte and I make our way to her flat in a taxi, and I have switched from army jargon to lovers' jargon. We talk of the future, of each other, her soulful dark eyes holding mine. Afterwards, fingers entwined and bodies glistening, we lie against each other until sleep settles over us, and quiet comes.

That night, I wake with orange streetlights on my face and half-sober drag my naked body from our warm bed, to stand by the curtainless window. I can see this first-floor room as a sangar, and for a minute I stand watching out at the usually busy street, waiting for a car to pass, listening to a rabble of party-goers weaving home along the kerbs.

I head to the fridge for a cold cider, and halfway through the bottle I find sleep again until the orange light has yielded to the day's brightness.

◊ ◊ ◊ ◊ ◊

In the final days of R&R my Plymouth visit is over. My father and I walk through the park in Yeovil almost in silence, with the dog yapping and dancing around. My father was a soldier himself, serving in embassies behind the Iron Curtain during the Cold War, and in Northern Ireland later in his career; and I can hear the unspoken worry in his voice when he asks casually whether I have had to fire my machinegun yet. I stare at the trees by the pond away in the distance. No, I tell him, we're not doing anything dangerous. Staying in camp, mostly. Very easy stuff. I am sure he doesn't believe me though. We walk on in silence, each painfully aware how little time we have left before I must return to Brize Norton.

◊ ◊ ◊ ◊ ◊

The days have sped by, and soon enough we are in Exeter — my girlfriend Charlotte, my parents, brother and I. Charlotte is getting the train back to Plymouth, and I am going to stay overnight with my parents before heading up to Brize Norton the next day.

The goodbye in the station car park is the worst of all. Charlotte is sobbing like I'm already dead, floods of tears streaming down her face as she shakes and holds my arm. I worry that she'll miss her train. She clings on to me as if she can keep me home by force. I feel the warmth of her skin, smell her perfume as she buries her head in my shoulder and cries into my jumper. It is too much; I try to deaden myself to it. I can't look at her, or speak, and so I hold her and wait for the train to come closer. The awful moment creeps nearer. After a few minutes of this I gently pry her away. My parents are waiting in the car just a few metres away.

'Charlotte,' I say gently, 'you have to go. You'll miss your train.'

She gulps and pulls her head away and we kiss, wet and salty from her tears, and she goes to leave but clings onto me again. It takes a few tries, but eventually she lets go. I wave to her, expressionless from the car window as she cries her way to the platform. Finally, she is gone from sight. I breathe a sigh of relief and relax a little, though the knot in my stomach is still there.

One the way back, new orders come by telephone. I am to report to Brize Norton straight away. I phone Peterson to ask if he's received the same news. A hire car is waiting for me at my parents' house. More tears, more goodbyes, I should be getting better at numbing myself to them. My efforts finally kick in on the drive back. I feel wooden, emotionless, like a machine.

I drive upcountry with the setting sun at my back, glimpsed in the reflected flash off cars I pass, until it is night, and the darkness of the road ahead draws me on. Petersen and I arrive back in Afghanistan the next night, and a Hercules transport aeroplane rattles us through the sky until we lurch to touch down in Bastion.

23. RAIN

Days pass, and more. Sleep comes with the dawn, or with dusk, or at midnight, and sometimes not at all. Our bodies protest, but we fill our bellies when we can, smoking Afghan cigarettes or ever-thinner roll ups between patrols, blowing out acrid haze into the moist air as the rain beats down. I am in the WMIK mostly, open to the air. When we wait in the vehicles before or after patrol, I sit on the floor of my WMIK, back to the ammunition racks, and close my eyes, imagining warm blue skies floating over the chalky downs of southern England. We can only wear thin gloves so as to be able to operate the GPMG, so my fingers are constantly numb.

Rain is everywhere, pooling in the ditches and runnels, dripping from the rim of our helmets, soaking our trousers until they cling to our skin and chafe us red raw over our thighs. When we sit on our cot beds before the sweet hours of sleep take us, our toes are candlewax-white and wrinkled from spending all patrol in wet boots. We dry the insides of our boots with balled up newspaper whilst we sleep, but the next day they will soak through again within minutes. The rain drums gently on the canvas tents as we sleep, spattering down on the metal frame of the WMIK and armour of the

Vector. It beads on my LMG then slithers off throughout the day, whilst she is propped against the ammunition racks by my right hand. There is no escape. The gas cylinder of my machine gun will be orange with rust every day, and it takes the better part of an hour to scrub every last rusty burr from her. When I sit on my cot bed, my chilled fingers flex slowly, I wriggle my toes when they are dried off and the feeling comes flooding back with warmth and pain. The rainy season is here, and we are at its mercy.

24. COBRAS, APACHES, LYNX

When we rise into the air, riding the desert winds to a FOB or contact to pick up a casualty, we never fly alone. Sometimes we are accompanied by a Lynx helicopter which acts as a vantage platform. An artillery observer is aboard, to call in smoke or fire missions if needed. Looking out of the porthole opposite, when I see a Lynx escorting us I relax slightly, as it means that chances are we're going to a FOB for an easy shout.

My throat, parched and dry from the adrenaline of being stood to, feels a nervous lump rise every time I see an AH-64 Apache rise into the air and fly with us. The hornet-like, sinister black gunship means trouble. Often, we lose sight of him early, as he will race to a contact ahead of us to get a strafing run in before we land. The Apache is awesome, terrifying, comforting and beautiful. When we land in contact and I see an Apache in the overhead, I feel a surge of elation, of safety, and we will them on, to kill, maim, destroy on our behalf as we take cover on the ground below.

Sea Cobras roam the overhead in pairs, manned by USMC pilots. They are our air support of choice when we are out on vehicle patrol in AO Robin, as they can be stood to quickly and there are more of them than there are

Apaches. The Cobras, like their namesakes, are fast and deadly, and we keep their frequencies scribbled and memorised and folded away in case we need to retune our radios to talk to them directly. We all know the words by heart.

'ECAS, ECAS, ECAS, I am not FAC trained — my position is…' and then tell them who you want them to kill.

During the first Gulf War, a number of British troops were killed by US air support, and mindful of the fact our vehicles look both ramshackle and armed, every man has an infrared light on his helmet, infrared lights inside bottles taped onto the HF antenna, reflective tape on our helmets and reflective chevrons on the wagons. The Cobras are fast and deadly, and we intend to stay alive.

25. SOND CHARA

Night sits all around us, swamp heavy blackness enveloping the vehicle patrol. We are sitting on the western side of the main wadi, high on the plains, watching the outskirts of Nad Ali through night vision goggles. Ngabo is watching our rear, and I am in the forward WMIK. The GPMG is dismounted and Bella is in the weapons mount; she can take a night vision scope, so for now she is at my shoulder whilst I observe the town spread out below us in a ghoulish jade vision.

42 Commando are conducting a clearance operation to flush the Taliban from their built-up fighting positions between Lashkar Gah and Nad Ali, pushing from the south to north in an unrelenting offensive named Sond Chara — Red Dagger in Pashto, to represent the red dagger insignia that all commandos cherish. The air is damp with recent rain, and the ground around us is churned up into mud by our tyres on the wet desert.

Between our two vehicles, one looking forward, one back, we have made an observation post of this jutting clifftop. Between us we will take note of any vehicle movements under cover of darkness, register where they move from and where they are going, to try and give intelligence to the Commando forces for when they have pushed through Nad Ali and to the canal.

There is no wind tonight, when the rains cleared earlier the breeze died, and sound carries far. From the central wadi village, a pair of dogs bark to each other, out of sight, and the vehicle commander turns outwards to his left slightly, watching up the wadi for any movement that could have spooked the dogs.

Ahead, in the green amplified light though my night vision scope, tracer fire rises into the sky, short bursts hosing the darkness with pricks of colour. I take my eye off the sight, and watch the green lights rise into the blackness to be quickly lost. But this is in the far distance, too far to even hear the sounds of weapon fire.

Sond Chara is the first major offensive of Herrick 9, and in the first day, yesterday, 42 Commando advanced on foot before pushing on to make contact with the enemy. They took ground through fierce fighting, bogged down in clinging mud but advancing through Taliban positions, and would continue to fight for days, steadily turning the screw and clearing the ground in Nad Ali.

◇ ◇ ◇ ◇ ◇

The night wears on, and no suspicious vehicles are seen. The fighting is too far to the south for our patrol to have gathered any useful intelligence, and with our radio batteries running low and bellies empty, we turn for Bastion. We patrol back slowly in the pre-dawn light, cautiously skirting a few compounds we come across that have scratched a small, basic irrigation system into a handful of fields. They will be growing opium poppy next season, but now the fields are bare and the farms silent.

Bastion rises up to meet our wheels, the familiar dust of camp settles on our wagons and weapons, and we hand over to the daytime patrol then make our way back to our tents, to sleep through the day as best we can until it is time for the next night's patrol.

A few days later, I am switched to day patrols. In the Vector, with Vince commanding, we roll up to the loading bay beside the front gate sangar, point our weapons in a safe direction: at the Hesco barrier in front of us. I pop open the gun, feeding a belt of linked ammunition into the body before slamming the cover down into place. Radios hum alive, EWD whir, and the patrol is ready. The Vector has a pair of GPMGs mounted fore and aft, one pointing ahead and one to the rear, with limited traverse. It is for this reason I prefer the WMIK, as although lighter than the Vector my gun turret can spin 360 degrees. I take my place in the forward top cover hatch, gun trained ahead, and we move out of the camp and onto Dasht-e Margo, the desert that starts at the base of the mountains to our north. A WMIK follows the Vector, racing wide to cover the flank, then ahead to clear junctions, like a satellite spinning around us as I mimic the reverse of the other top cover's arc, our GPMGs always pointing opposite. I duck inside the body of the vehicle, emerge again at the rear top cover hatch when the WMIK points ahead, and duck back when we have the lead.

We make our way over the rolling stone dunes at the wadi edge, WMIK on a flank and I pointing out towards the wadi, when from the dull landscape something catches my eye. A glint that has no right to be there.

I call over the patrol radio. 'Something out to the right. IED indicator maybe.'

Vince stops the patrol, the WMIK top cover and commander provide all-round defence and I duck down from my gun to crouch inside the armoured wagon, explaining to Vince what I saw, how far away it was, what colour, what size. My heart is pounding and doubt rises within me that it's nothing, or something obvious, that I've stopped us for no reason, and the laughter and jokes of the patrol will be turned on me that night for my naïveté.

Vince steps out of the commander's seat and makes his

way to the troop hatch at the back of the Vector, climbs inside, sticks a head out of the hatch next to me, and from his new vantage point sweeps the ground with binoculars. He sees the glint too, maybe two hundred metres away, at the base of a dune in a dried-up floodwater runnel. We are to investigate; Vince thinks it may be a come on, a trap to lure us into an IED or an ambush, although by now I'm sure it's nothing. In obedience to Vince's heightened alertness, I cock my GPMG anyway, thumb on the safety catch and I am ready to fire. The WMIK circles around onto a patch of high ground, with good visibility, and provides all-round defence. Our Vector moves back to approach the glint from mid slope, avoiding the obvious route and the low ground. We creep closer. I can just about make out the blue metallic sheen and distinctive fin shape of a mortar bomb — no, a pair of bombs — as Vince calls over the patrol net to tell us the same. Relief and excitement taste hot in my mouth — I was right! We stop, and now Vince plucks the HF handset to his ear and calls Zero to send a 'ten liner', a request for bomb disposal assistance sent in strict form.

Why two bombs? One could be a fired round that didn't explode, but two bombs, lying next to each other, aligned neatly, and pointing towards Bastion? Someone has put these here, either as a cache or as part of an IED.

Vince needs to clear the area so that an ATO can be dispatched to investigate. I watch from my gun as Bruce Lee steps out of his vehicle with an Ebex, a battered old metal detector that is already obsolete, and starts clearing an area for the EOD command and control vehicle to occupy whilst they investigate. Mine tape and tent pegs mark the corners of the box he clears, and before long the task is complete, and we are waiting in position for the bomb disposal team to arrive. The desert is quiet and still, a lone buzzard floats on air currents in the distance as I watch towards Nad Ali. The wind stirs dust into life in puffs and eddies that quickly fade and die, dropping the sand back down to the desert with a sigh. We shift and stretch, flex fingers and twist our backs against body armour. We are good at waiting; we have had plenty of practice — and will have plenty more before our deployment is over.

ATO are escorted out of camp by the other vehicle patrol, and a pair of Vixens pull up beside us in the newly cleared command and control area. It feels unusual to have so many troops out here with us, instead of the usual six strong patrol, and I relax slightly as they arrive. Finally, with fourteen men, four vehicles, and six GPMGs we have enough strength to call ourselves a small vehicle patrol. But a knot rises in my stomach within a few minutes, as we are to push on and let the pair of Vixens of the other patrol handle the ATO tasking. We are needed to sweep an area underneath the flight path into Bastion, to deter any Taliban with RPGs or Stinger missiles from trying to down our aircraft. And with that, we are off. The wheels turn, and our patrol moves on, eyes on the desert, my mortar find forgotten and thoughts on the next task.

26. THE ROAD TO HELMAND (CONTINUED)

The night wind blusters, and rain lashes my cheek as I take another cautious step. We are clearing the road towards the north for the resupply convoy, sweeping for mines and bombs. Unlike mine, Litch's metal detector seems to be working — twice now he has called a stop, after red-light suspicions raised from his control panel. Both times I stop on the dirt road, sling my Vallon over my back and unhook Bella from her straps, watching my machine-gun arc and waiting.

The road surface is swimming now with run-off water, and Litch digs deep with an entrenching spade until he finds the metallic source. Each time, he has called over the radio that we are clear to continue, and I swap Bella for the Vallon again and against my desire, take another step. The vehicle behind sticks close in our tracks, engine throbbing and water vapour lifting off from around the bonnet as the heat of the engine meet the rains that are falling all around us.

◊ ◊ ◊ ◊

I am lost, swimming in the depths of myself in a pool of my mind so deep I can't imagine ever coming back. I have never been so aware of the frailty of my life, of the relentless march of time, and how every road we walk ends in death. It seems bizarre, like I've been sleepwalking my whole life, never really understanding the inescapable truth that one day, I will die. That everything I have ever been will be reduced back to dust, my dreams and memories — my loves, my mistakes, the lessons I have learned, my triumph and shames and fears, will all cease to be. And I have no power — none — over when that day will come.

I take another step, my stomach knotted as my weight transfers and the dirt crunches under my boot. The flash, the heat, the blast of shrapnel that I expect doesn't come this step. Or the next.

◊ ◊ ◊ ◊ ◊

The wind drops suddenly, and I raise my head a little, although the rain still falls. The ditches to the side of the road are lost, replaced by dunes and hummocks barely visible in the yellow glare. We are approaching the junction with Highway One. I know I should be relieved that our task is nearing completion, but the closer we are the more dangerous the IED risk. Litch slows down, and I have time between steps to take a breath and blow out ragged, shaking air that mists around my head. The convoy is stopped now, a protection team has moved through the dunes, around us onto the hard tarmac of Highway One, and is waiting for Litch and I. All we have to do is make it onto the tarmac and off the dirt road. My newfound mortality steps with me as we heave closer, then finally, the last agonising steps where I plead again silently for another day of life.

And then — then, it is all over. I have stepped onto the tarmac, and I am still here, still alive. Almost instantly, a foolish grin splits my face as I think of my prayers through the night with embarrassment. Litch throws back his head and pumps a silent fist to the sky, then slings his Vallon and swaggers over to the WMIK. I clamber back into the

Vector, puff-faced and bloodshot, my body weary to the core, still wet and aching.

The rain stopped just before dawn and the light blue ink wash of the eastern sky has flooded the night out, even the last stars of the western sky have dimmed their lamps when we turn about to drive back into camp. The convoy has gone; passed out of sight, rumbling through the cool morning mists towards Gereshk, whilst we watched the junction. Griff swivels from his seat up front and calls back to me. 'Well done today Addy.'

I know better though. I was lucky.

27. FALLING ASLEEP

Weariness rests about me like a blanket, dogging my every turn. Limbs are so tired that every movement is an effort. Eyes slip closed without warning. Hour by hour, I fight the growing urge to relax, to stop looking for IEDs and ranging firing points. I have been struggling through patrol for the past fourteen hours, from midday heat to small-hour's chill.

As the patrol ends, I stagger from the transport yard after we have handed over the vehicles to the outgoing patrol. The polluted haze of Bastion's nightscape glows silently as we trudge back to Wyvern Lines. The pall of smoke from the burn pits away on the northern edge of camp settles back on Bastion, falling around the staccato, orange lights that punctuate the skyline. The mountains fade away into the vastness of the empty night until all that my eyes can see, squinting and blinking, are dancing dust-shapes flooding down around the glare of the lamp lights. We make our way back to the lines, skirting around the edge of dirt-roads until the familiar dust of our company lines crunches under our feet again.

My armour is shed with a tearing open of Velcro straps, and the cool air brings a shiver as it floods across my sweat-damp shoulders. I prop the armour plates by my cot, and my helmet, weapon and ammo will be laid out in readiness too in case of night-time attack. I sigh and stretch, not yet able to rest. There is still work yet to do. I wipe down Bella, the day's dust turning into an orange grime as it mixes with the gun oil on the muzzle and around the magazine housing. I unclip the 100-round box of link still on Bella's body, and stow it in my haversack of rounds with the rest of my ammunition and grenades. Drying off the remaining oil in her body takes longer, and as I do so, Vince strolls up.

'Addy,' he calls out, and pushes my shemagh aside. 'Did you get any mail?' He is wearing only boxers, sandals and a Father Christmas hat, but his face is lined with the happy grin of someone who has had a wash and cleaned their teeth and is ready for a few hours of rest. I hadn't had time to read them yet, but two letters have been delivered to my cot, and are waiting on my pillow.

'Yeah, a few. I'll open them in a sec,' I say, and finish tending to Bella, propping her on her bipod and shoulder strap by my bed, a shemagh over her to keep the dust off.

Vince hovers over me whilst I open my mail. The first letter is a Christmas card from Corporal T back home, our storeman from the Bloody Eleventh, which is signed by him and his wife. I read the short message inside and pass the card to Vince. Sharing mail is common unless it comes from wives or sweethearts. Vince reads the message too, then hangs the card with the few others I have already acquired on a length of cord strung across my cubicle space, along one wall.

'You did well today, Addy,' he says, an echo of Griff from a few days before. 'Get some sleep, I'll wake you for lunch if you want.'

He swishes out of my bedspace, and I shed my dusty uniform, swapping desert cam for boxers and sandals. The

120

pre-dawn air chills me quickly as I step out of the tent towards the wash block to rinse my puffed face and wind-chapped lips. I clean fuzzy teeth, blowing out clouds of white foam into the sink. Then I shave ready for tomorrow and examine my bloodshot eyes. Only after preparing for bed do I sneak back to a darkened tent to read my letter from Charlotte by torchlight, and, once finished, I twist the torch off, still smiling. A haze of sleep falls quickly, marking off another day for the British Army in Afghanistan, and another day closer to home.

28. RIFLEMAN NASH DIES

Christmas week has come, and the stars dance overhead in the cold empty sky, spinning away the final few hours until my sentry duty whilst, oblivious to their rise, I slumber sound. Sound in my sleeping bag that engulfs me like warm, empty death. Sound through the lonely hours that my comrades sit on sentry, eking out the minutes like a miser. I sleep sound, even through the dust-whipped din of a Chinook touching down outside the hospital in the small hours. Rifleman Nash, and I, sleep on.

We arrived at FOB Tombstone four days ago, bouncing across the dirt packed road in Snatch Land Rovers. Our small convoy crosses the two kilometres or so between Bastion and FOB Tombstone in a few minutes. I am riding snugly in the back with Vince, whilst a top cover, legs straddling the back seats, sticks his head and shoulders out of the top of the vehicle, his weapon stock snug in his shoulder, ready for trouble. Vince and I haven't even bothered loading our weapons, and a belt of link hangs limp and weary from my 100-round box, as Bella rests muzzle down between my legs. Vince's helmet rattles around on the empty seat next to him. Shafts of sunlight feint and weave around us, spilling in past the top cover, as we make our way to a week of sentry at FOB Tombstone. No-one is really looking forward to the prospect but, like anything in the army, things could be worse, and we always remember that.

We take up quarters in an old building that had been sub-divided down into dormitory-style cubicles by plywood boards, which are empty save for one issue mattress laid out on one cot bed per cubicle. There is an admin area at the front of the building nearest the main gate, with a desk, tv, several chairs and most importantly of all a brew station.

Griff and the Lance Corporals receive a handover brief from the off-going team, and quickly work out a roster. We each have four hours on overwatch in the guard tower overlooking the main gate, then four hours standing at the main gate checking passes and opening and closing the gate, then twelve hours off. I start with four hours off, and sit with the Corporals in the admin area watching grainy DVDs, episode after episode, cup of tea after cup of tea, until dusk creeps in and it is my turn for duty in the tower. I make my way to the gun position layered up for the cold, with my shemagh wrapped around my neck to keep the chill off. I haul my way up the metal ladder to a portacabin on stilts overlooking the main gate, and the Bastion road.

Litch is lounging on the chair at the top, feet up, magazine in hand, radio on. He gave up watching the road minutes into his stag. Barbed wire-topped sandbags ring the sliding window that fronts our watchpost, and the GPMG noses blindly out into the night beyond. We do a quick handover, which consists of Litch telling me how bored he is. Then, he departs and leaves me to huddle into my own warmth, hunched and stooped on the chair, sitting, watching out into the night. The radio plays tinny BFBS tunes and the night drags by, minute after minute inexorably bringing us closer to the next hour, and the next, until eventually the final minutes of my sentry will drag out painfully slowly, and my own relief will come up the ladder and listen to me tell him how bored I am.

Days pass as we move from sangar to gate to plywood sleeping box. Sometimes we kick our way through the dust to the cookhouse to eat greasy, cold food under sterile lighting, otherwise we keep ourselves fed on tea and biscuits between sentry. There are no officers here, just a Corporal in charge of the gate. Afghans come and go; interpreters come into the camp, as do the local traders who have set up a market for the troops just outside the gate. Passes are checked, vehicles searched, and wary, ever wary of a suicide bomber driving up, we stand shuffling our feet and impatiently will away the time until sentry change out.

We all prefer the night, when we lock the camp gates up and watch over from on high, instead of standing outside like a security guard, playing Russian roulette with each Afghan vehicle that drives up to us and stops.

On this particular night, I am sleeping sound, whilst a Chinook brings the body of Rifleman Nash to Bastion from his Patrol Base that he fought from. The first Rifleman to die on Herrick 9, and it's not yet Christmas. The Chinook touched down outside the hospital, waspish nurses buzz around the corridors and the wounded are processed by name and number.

◊ ◊ ◊ ◊ ◊

By the time I have woken, the mood in our small camp of Riflemen has soured, the laughter and shouts across the cookhouse are gone, instead there is only isolation whilst the dead man's family are told the news. Phones are shut off, an electronic drawing down of blinds whilst the visiting officers back home make the longest walk from car to front door.

News filters through to us: he took a fatal gunshot wound during an attack on a Taliban position. The Christmas letter from his family has already gone out, a care package with a hand-written note of mother's love is still in air-freight to camp; and I have a stone in my stomach as I sit on sentry later that morning, watching his friends and comrades practising the coffin carry for the remembrance service we will hold after Christmas. Up and down they march, towards an ambulance with a dummy coffin, they take it on their shoulders, march away, stop, reset, and repeat. The RSM drills them over and over, so that they won't falter when it comes to the final task they'll perform for their friend. Eventually the RSM is content, and the soldiers in the square below my sangar fit their berets behind their belt straps and fall out.

In my maudlin way, I wonder how I would cope in my final moments, had that been me to fall instead of him. Would the pain be very great, or would the shock numb me to everything, except a gentle falling asleep? Would I be resigned, or frantic with regret for the pain my family are about to go through because of my dying?

I wonder on this as the unexpected calm and warm day filters bright yellow light into the sangar, and the radio spits out tinny tunes. I dip biscuit after biscuit in my thermos tea and munch my way through hours of watching down a gunsight.

29. CHRISTMAS AT FOB TOMBSTONE

Christmas Day comes around, the midnight air moist with the threat of rain, visibility close around us. I am shivering my way through the night at FOB Tombstone on top sangar, radio and machine gun for company. Festive pop songs play softly on BFBS in the background as, eyes on the Shorabak road, my mind conjures pictures for me of the coming morning's celebrations back home. My brother, the excitement of his recent childhood still on him, smiling as he makes his way through his presents. My father, nonchalant as ever, wearing a paper crown and garish new Christmas jumper. My mother and sister to-ing and fro-ing in the kitchen, stopping every so often for a quick top up of the sherry glass as the smell of basting and roasting wafts around. And Charlotte. What will she be doing? We have never known a Christmas together, my mind is blank when I try to imagine her amongst the close-knit family of hers, their quirks and traditions.

My attention is pulled back to the present, when the radio — HF, not BFBS — crackles.

'Zero this is Granite 64.' Ah, that's Chalky, over in Bastion main sangar. What do they want?

'Suspicious personnel spotted in my location. Over.'

Zero wants to know more. 'Can you give a description of what's happening?'

'One person in a very suspicious vehicle.'

Zero knows by now what is happening and asks for an A to H description. Chalky is happy to oblige:

'Alpha: old. Bravo: fat. Charlie: red. Delta: jolly. Break. Interrogative, roger so far?'

Zero again: 'Roger so far.'

'Echo: short. Foxtrot: chubby. Golf: with a sack. Hotel: white.'

Zero: 'Did he leave any presents?'

'Granite 64, negative, we've been naughty.'

'Zero roger out.'

An hour or so later, and my watch is done for the night. Bruce Lee relieves me, and I return to my plywood cubicle, to grab a few hours of sleep before the morning light comes and the camp wakes for the new day. A dreamless slumber takes me, and Christmas steals in as I am asleep.

◊ ◊ ◊ ◊ ◊

There is a long-standing British army tradition in which the enlisted men are served their Christmas meal by officers. So it is in FOB Tombstone. As I come off rest to man the main gate, I find the entranceway of our accommodation blocked by a pair of officers. The RSM and the CO. They are standing silently, disapprovingly in the doorway. The RSM is holding a tray with a bread roll in it. One left, which must be mine. I walk toward them, smile, take the bread roll. It has a sausage in it.

'Thank you, sir,' I say, and step back.

Vince, sitting in the duty NCO desk, is just finishing his as I arrive. The other men have all finished their sausage baps and retired to their bunks or their duty. Silence reigns. The office is empty but for the RSM, the CO, Vince and I. They are all waiting for me to eat. Three pairs of eyes watch the journey of bun to mouth. I chew, chew, chew. The rolls were prepared in a hurry, there is scant butter. My dry mouth refuses to cooperate and it takes me several tries to swallow the first enormous globules of half-chewed bread and burnt sausage. Finally, a wad slides painfully down my gullet, and my mouth is empty. I look down at my breakfast. The large roll has one small bite taken out of it. Three pairs of eyes watch the journey of bun to mouth again. After what seems like an age and the most awkward, odd breakfast I have ever experienced, I am without a bread roll. The RSM and CO swivel like on greased bearings to disappear back through the door without a word.

Vince spins his chair around and raises he eyebrows, half shrugging and frowning at the same time. 'Well, that was weird.' His appraisal of the situation is right. 'Merry Christmas by the way Addy. Have you heard the good news?'

I haven't.

'Half of us are going back to Bastion. 1 Platoon are going on foot patrol across the eastern wadi, we're filling in. You've got twenty-four hours on the airfield sangar. Transport leaves this afternoon.'

I spend Christmas morning on the main gate, stopping the battered cars that come towards me, checking passes of the civilian contractors coming into the FOB, and raising and lowering the barrier for them as they pass through. The Afghan men coming in dribs and drabs are a strange bunch. Handspun woollen jumpers cover them, thin blankets across their shoulders, and thinner cotton trousers complete the ensemble. All wear beards. Some chew tobacco widely and frown their stained teeth at me as they proffer their identity cards. Others greet me with a wide smile and a gentle handshake as if we are old friends. Their lives are written stark on their faces for all to see, their eyes bright under bushy eyebrows, their faces creased and lined by years of windswept toil on Helmand's dusty plain.

The hours wear on, and in ones and twos battered cars

park up by Shorabak and divest themselves of Afghans. Little by little, blankets are spread out and wares placed on show. The locals are having their weekly bazaar. The thinking is that by allowing the economy to grow outside of opium production, ISAF will wean the Nad Ali locality off Taliban control — and this starts with an ISAF approved, drug-free bazaar right under our noses.

My watch is over, and Vince comes out to greet me along with my relief. He is armoured up, with his weapon clipped casually to his chest, hanging down.

'Fancy it, Addy?'

I don't, but Vince can't go alone and I suspect that the question isn't really a question at all. Vince wants to practise his Pashto, win some hearts and minds, make friends, and do his bit to show these Pashtun men that we are not the monsters that we imagine they imagine us as. I suspect that this is a fool's errand, that we will be best friends for as long as they have something to gain from it; and after the last dollar has been spent any loyalty to ISAF or our mission will be as disposable as the wealth which we seem to be pouring into this province. I check Bella's magazine is seated and set off with Vince to the bazaar in front of camp.

◊ ◊ ◊ ◊ ◊

The Afghans have a saying: me against my brother, my brothers and I against our father, our family against our neighbours, our tribe against everyone else. I suspect that the line about 'our tribe and ISAF against the Taliban' which our commanders are trying to write in doesn't have an equivalent in Pashto. Even with my basic Rifleman's knowledge though, I can see the flaws in the strategy. To be sure there is grand reasoning, cooked up by clever men far away, focussing on detailed predications about provincial economics, years of counter-insurgency strategy from Malaya to Ireland. But no matter what we might do there is always the tribalism, the hierarchy of loyalty, now a united tribe and then in a heartbeat: brothers set against father, the uniting against outsiders but turning on themselves when the outsiders are gone — this is Afghanistan, a civil war we can never win because we are not a part of any Afghan identity. We will always be the furthest outside of that proverb, the foreign infidel against whom every Afghan must unite. Asking Pashtun to unite with ISAF against Pashtun is asking them to turn their tradition on its head.

We stroll through the bazaar, salaams quick on our lips but Bella is cocked and ready. Vince stops in front of a battered Toyota Corolla and shakes hands in turn with a pair of men squatting on their haunches beside a blanket covered in brass trinkets, bells, and cymbals. He chats amiably in his rudimentary Pashto, and the elder man replies in short sentences, juggling his hand, rolling it in the air as he does.

Keen to try my hand at this game we call hearts and minds, I stop at the next blanket where only a single young man is showing his wares. He has blankets, rugs, all sorts of wools. I smile and salaam, taking a hand off Bella and placing it over my chest to show my sincerity. I hear my father's voice in my head as I do so, 'Always be sincere, whether you mean it or not!' A quick 'Alykum salaam' returns to me, and without the Pashto skills of Vince, I must rely on basics.

I stumblingly rattle off the only sentence I remember from our phrase book. The stall owner nods, then he asks if I am enjoying my visit to his homeland. His English is better than my Pashto. Of course it is, he has had three years of ISAF, I have only had three months of Helmand. I would rather talk economics and industry instead of politics and travel, and I ask where the rugs are made. He grabs a bundle into his arms and starts throwing them down into the blanket as he speaks.

'This one, Balochi pattern. This one, Pashtun. This one,

Pashtun. This one, Balochi. This one, Iran.' This one, this one, this one. Like flipping through a catalogue, rugs are thrown out on display for the briefest second before the next one lands on top of it, and he shows me every single rug he owns and tells me where is comes from. 'Which ones do you buy?'

Very clever, and now I am on the spot. I choose a small square Balochi pattern. He chides me. 'Very nice, very good, but small. Small. A man like you must have big rug for your big house. Come, you must have more.'

I don't have a house, but Vince reminds me, 'These go for double the price on eBay. You could buy a couple and then sell when you get home.'

Dollar signs writ large in my mind now, I choose a pair of larger ones, Pashtun patterns.

The stall holder presses on. 'Yes, yes, good. So this is one hundred twenty dollars, a good price for you I think.'

We start negotiating, and I drive a hard bargain — as far as I can tell — and the stall holder will leave later that day ninety dollars richer. As I turn to leave, I want to give him a show of respect for his hard negotiating, to show in front of all the bazaar that I appreciate his goods and his stall. I feel the wool of a Pashtun hat, smiling and giving a thumbs up.

He insists on carrying my new rugs back to the FOB Tombstone gate for me, and Vince and I make our way back to camp. Before we part, my new rug salesman has a present for me: the hat that I admired. Hand over my heart in earnest this time, eyes wide, I tell him that I cannot accept such a generous gift, but he insists. The interpreter on the main gate says something to him in Pashto, and he replies.

The interpreter advises me, 'You must take it.'

I do so, and try to offer some money, thirty dollars, making my earlier negotiation pointless, but the stallholder will not accept. We part ways forever, and he leaves. Before I go into camp, our interpreter has an Afghan cultural lesson for me.

'You must never admire something that belongs to another man. If someone admired something of yours, you must give it to him. It is our culture.'

Lunchtime consists of stale biscuits and tea; the cookhouse is closed whilst chefs prepare the FOB Tombstone Christmas supper. When I have dipped and swirled and eaten, I retire to my bunk to try and catch some sleep — get in my time machine, as Chris put it — to try and fast forward a few hours until the transport for Bastion and sangar duty leaves.

◇ ◇ ◇ ◇ ◇

Bleary hours later, I am bounced around in the back of a Vector, rattling across the roads back to Bastion. We pass into camp, and head past ones and twos of soldiers making their way out of the cookhouse. Bastion Christmas lunch has dragged on, it seems.

We round the camp to the airfield, and the expanse of the desert opens up from the false neighbourliness of the camp, showing us distance, space. Emptiness. A vast black gulf lies between sangars here on the edge of the airfield, a kilometre or more from the camp proper, half that between sangars. My fellow sentry Corporal Ozzy and I will be by ourselves in this fortress tower for twenty-four hours. We will lock ourselves into the cage surrounding it, and then double bolt the thick steel door behind us, retreating into a prison of safety. As we lock the off-going sentries out and ourselves in, Bazza has a quiet word with me.

'I left something for you. By the gun. For both of you. Merry Christmas.'

I make my way up to the third floor and the lookout tower for first watch, whilst Corporal Ozzy settles down into his cot bed on the second floor for four hours of rest to start the duty. There is a fruit juice bottle next to the gun, half empty. Probably just less than a quarter pint left. I waft the bottle in front of my nose — brandy.

The hours wear on. I steep some noodles in boiling water, and too impatient to let them soften, crunch my way through a watery supper. Five minutes before Corporal Ozzy relives me, I grab the bottle and with a silent salute to the desert in front of me, drink the lot. The next four hours pass by as if I were in a time machine, for I sleep sound, and content.

30. STITCHED UP

I have barely placed my head on the pillow after a long night patrol and closed my eyes when a rude hand shakes me roughly awake, and I am dazzled as I come to.

'Addy. You've lost a whole bloody magazine, mate. Come to the work yard now.'

'What?' I wake slowly, even though the next patrol has not yet gone out. It is half an hour since I was stood down. 'I have a Minimi. Her mags are in my ammo pouch.'

The torch in my face is unrelenting. 'Work yard. Now.'

I slip my sandals on, pull a combat shirt over my head and wrap a shemagh about my neck to keep the cold at bay. By the time I have walked halfway to the work yard, I am wide awake and seething. I report to the Corporal who oversees the next patrol. He gets straight down to business.

'This pistol was in the back of your wagon.' He gesticulates with a SIG P226 held loosely by the trigger guard. 'It's empty. No mag. Where's the magazine?'

I inherited a loaded pistol when I took over the patrol thirteen hours ago. As usual, I checked the pistol was made safe, with a magazine attached, then stowed it safely in my combat pocket, and would have handed it over to the next patrol untouched, except...

'Except that's not my pistol. Litch, the vehicle commander, took it from me when we stopped at the end of our shift. He said he needed to check everything was there before handover.'

The Corporal, like any good infantry soldier, is like a terrier and unable to let go of one idea until he has his teeth prized from it. 'It was in the back of your wagon. It's your responsibility.'

I try another tack. 'There was a magazine in it when I handed it to Litch. I didn't see it after that. If it was in the back of the wagon when you took over, he must have placed it there himself.'

Corporal Terrier is nearly catching on. 'Ok, so if you say that Litch took it from you, why would he have taken the magazine out?'

I don't know for sure, but I have a suspicion. 'Have you tried looking for the magazine in the wagon?' I ask.

'Of course,' pipes up the top cover. 'It's not anywhere back here.'

I have another idea though. 'There was a magazine in the pistol Litch gave you, that will be the magazine he took from my pistol. He lost his magazine and stole mine to cover his arse. Try looking all in the front of the wagon. The footwell, the seats — everywhere.'

Corporal Terrier looks incensed at the idea of taking a suggestion from a Rifleman. The top cover slides across the bars into the front seat, and a few seconds later calls out 'Got it!' It was wedged behind the commander's seat. Litch must have accidently knocked the magazine release catch, and the magazine dropped out of his pistol. Unfazed by losing live rounds, he simply decided to steal mine and hope that no-one noticed. I turn back for lines, anger coursing through me.

The next morning Litch denies stealing the magazine, laughing with Chalky and Andy and turning my righteous anger at his theft into a joke for all the platoon. I leave them to their laughter, and sit by myself, dejected, on the Hesco barrier by the interpreters' tent. I gaze out towards the airfield sangars, standing in the distance.

Jamshed joins me, and lights a cigar, puffing at it and blowing sparks off the tip. He stands beside me for a minute, like me in silence. He can see something is amiss and tries his best to plough on into conversation.

'Do not fear,' he says, pointing to the sky with a thin finger, the wisdom of his youth pulled up proud for all the world to see. 'Do not fear. Allah has a plan for you. You will see.'

Grateful for the company, I listen in silence and Jamshed pretends not to notice the one-way conversation whilst he tells me of his village, and his brothers, and their plans for a farm that they will buy together one day.

31. MREs

It is night, and the year is nearly over. Our patrol has come up against fortress Bastion, a ring of concrete and razor wire that in under a year's time, the Taliban will penetrate under the noses of the RAF Regiment. We patrol outside the camp at all hours, sometimes bright, headlights dazzling, confident under the cover of the sangar machine guns, to show we are here. Sometime we patrol 'dark', with IR lights on and the top covers' eyes wide by moonlight, watching for any suspicious vehicles creeping by with their lights off. And so, as both an overt deterrent and a covert security force, we spend seemingly endless nights, outside the wire, roaming and circling. Tonight though, we are the ones up to no good. We have come up against fortress Bastion, and we intend to win.

We are at the gate to Bastion 2, the first extension of Bastion, away to the south side of the airfield. They are already drawing up plans for Bastion 7, but that is the future. Here in the present at Bastion 2 is a gate manned by US Forces — 'The Yanks.' Our patrol is supposed to come through the main gate, but here we are on the doorstep. There is one problem though — they won't let us in. The drivers honk their horns, flash their lights, and Vince gets out of the commander's side to shout up to the sangar.

'Friendlies coming in mate, open up!'

'Gate's locked till tomorrow,' comes the response (it already is tomorrow, but the sentry must be going off watch soon, tomorrow will be after he has woken up, therefore it must still be today in his eyes).

Vince, although he knows this, feigns astonishment. 'Let us in, we're low on fuel, we can't break down out here, we'd be stranded!'

Ah, The British are in trouble! Never fear, Yanks to the rescue! This does the job, and now, status quo restored and America the saviour again of us the junior partner, the gate opens. We drive in, up-thumbing our grateful thanks to the sentries behind their guns, and casting glances around us as we do so. Lights on, engines purring hoarsely, we drive through Bastion 2 towards the main camp.

But what's this? As we approach the internal gateway that separates American Bastion from other ISAF troops, we go dark. Lights are dead, top covers drop down inside the vehicle, remove our helmets and stow our weapons. Slowly, quietly, we snake around the dark internal perimeter road, still within the American sector, and stealthily circle round. Close inside the gate again, at a point the patrol commander identified when we came through, the top covers jump out and saunter over to the palettes of supplies stored underneath the sangar watchtowers. As long as we are silent, we are safe.

Knives in hand, Conlay and I cut through cargo straps and shrink wrap to reveal boxes of MREs — meals ready to eat — the American rations. Vehicle commanders join us, and armfuls are carried hastily back to the Vector, the larger of the two wagons. I climb back into the WMIK silently and give Andy a knock on the back of his seat to let him know I'm back. Seconds later, the Vector moves off, and we follow. Silence gives way to elation as we approach Wyvern Lines.

'Hahaa, look at all this!'

Our unit stopped issuing rations a week ago due to supply shortages, and with over half our deployment remaining we are left to fend for ourselves. Patrols passed hungrily, as our platoon ate its way through the food packages sent to us by civilians at home. Then, patrols passed angrily, for those of us without food stashed away from welfare packages, when the communal well ran dry.

Yesterday someone swapped a desert combat smock for six MREs, and in the dawning realisation that the Americans had more food than they wanted or needed, Operation Bellyful was born.

◊ ◊ ◊ ◊ ◊

Back at Wyvern Lines, we hide our gleeful cargo, dividing them up. Most find their way into the communal boxes in the entranceway to our tent, but we each keep a respectable personal supply stashed away. With our patrols over, both our airfield patrol and the mission for MREs, I sleep quickly, waking only a few times to drop my hand down and check Bella is still there beside my cot. Morning comes, and a briefing from the boss.

'Someone stole MREs in the night- you wouldn't know anything about that would you?' Of course we don't, and of course he knows it was us. 'I don't want to hear any more reports like this.'

He won't. We took enough to last until the end of deployment.

32. NEW YEAR'S DAY 2009

I RT this is Ops.'

The radio crackles, and the IRT team springs into action — weapons and ammo, armour and bodies, racing hearts and dry mouths collide at the flight line. The shout went out, but of all this I knew nothing, I heard nothing. Vince and I were on the 'ready' team, but Vince was needed to drive and pick some supplies up, and I went with him to lug ammo boxes to Wyvern Lines.

We arrived back at the IRT tent ten minutes later, to find the place half empty; the second team had taken the call and gone out, in our place. Annoyed at missing a shout, we check our weapons and kit more for something to do than any real need. My backpack has a number of pouches into which hand grenades, smoke grenades, mini flares, link, more link, coiled link, field dressings and tourniquets, and yet more link are all stored in their own place. Most of the extra link is for the 7.62mm GPMG, all Bella's 5.56mm link hangs in a pouch at my left hip, unboxed and hanging loose in belts, ready to be fed and fired. I check all my kit, then settle down on my cot.

Half an hour passes, and then the radio crackles again.

'IRT2, IRT1. At flight line. Over.' This is the call for Big

Jimmy to jump in the wagon and go and pick up the team that just went out to fetch a casualty. I go with him, to help carry EWD and the lads' kit. We speed through the camp, taking right-angled corners at speed (the roads are all built on a grid system of regimental straight lines) until we arrive at the Chinook pan. Pulling up behind the helicopter, engines cooling and rotors already stopped, something is instantly amiss. The Riflemen we are collecting are standing, kit at their feet, not a word passing between them nor smile to crack through the pall of shock and anger.

'Bad one guys?' Big Jimmy asks.

Richards just shakes his head slowly, looking at the ground, lips pursed. He can't talk about it, although I don't yet understand why.

◊ ◊ ◊ ◊ ◊

We drive back to the tent in silence. I jump out the back of the Land Rover first and we unload kit, radios and EWD, hauling the backpacks toward the tent. It must have been a casualty in a bad way, I expect. Richards is still too shaken up to say anything, but I'm sure everything will return to normal and the world will be as it was. As I haul kit, Richards and Bazza are conferring, standing side by side a little way off, watching us unload. Then Richards comes over.

'Addy, a word.'

I stop on the dusty walkway, just outside the entrance to the tent. The IRT team has already disappeared inside.

Richards continues. 'We're not supposed to say anything until Op Minimise comes on. But since you knew him, I think you should know. It was Chris we picked up today.'

My heart lurches — Chris is in camp! He'll be in the hospital, I'll have to visit before he is moved to the military hospital in Birmingham, he'll have to delay the wedding until he is better, of course.

Richards hasn't finished though. 'IED. Hit his vehicle.

He died instantly.'

I hear the words, but somehow, like the wrong jigsaw piece, they don't fit. The sun is still shining, I am still here, everything is the same as it was. The world isn't rendered in half, no bolt of lightning hits — Chris is dead. I hear and understand, waiting for grief to bubble up inside me.

Richards again, 'Can you hang back while I tell the chaps inside the tent please. They don't yet know.'

Yes, I can hang back. Richards has to tell the chaps inside the tent, as they don't yet know. He walks in. I carry an EWD to the entranceway and stand it on its end on a cot bed. Then another EWD is laid next to it, and another, just like it was this morning when Chris was alive. I kneel by the cot bed, eyes on my task, stacking the three EWD into neat lines, red, white, blue, propped up against each other. Then I take them off again and restack them, blue, white, red. Stack the EWD. Chris is dead. Restack the EWD. Tug on the EWD straps and tighten the buckles. Chris is dead. I kneel like at communion, head bowed, going over and over in my mind what has just happened. I am calm, lucid, waiting for tears to fight back, waiting for denial, anger, bargaining — still nothing. Just emptiness, a desert-wide expanse of nothing.

What sort of monster have I made of myself, that my friend dies, and I can't find a tear? I make my way back into the tent. There are tears in here, Fisk's eyes are red and his cheeks puffed. Vince is standing by the doorway, he rests a hand on my shoulder, and guides me to my cot. Hot, sweet tea is what I need, they have decided, and a steaming brew stands at the foot of my cot. Details pass in front of me like a train streaking through a station. It was a vehicle patrol with Chris in the lead WMIK, the IED blast killed two men and seriously wounded a third, the memorial service would be held at FOB Tombstone.

A few hours later, when dusk is drawing down and the helicopter engine roar from the flight line has given way to rumbling lorries outside the lines, Richards takes me aside once more. Do I need a rest? He can give me a few admin days if I need them. Each man of the Bloody Eleventh was offered before me, and all of them declined. The question hangs in air, with the expected answer hanging heavier.

'No thanks Richards. I just want to crack on; get on with the job.'

The Job — can you distil purpose into any of this? Of course, we patrol to keep the camp safe. We patrol to show the locals they can trust us over the Taliban. We patrol to gather intelligence. We patrol for this reason, for that reason, for all the reasons under the sun. We pick up casualties because they are wounded and need aid. Each facet of our tasking, broken down to bare bones, makes perfect sense. And when you put all that perfect sense together you get The Job. The thing that I have just professed I want to crack on with and do.

'Good man,' says Richards, and he turns away.

And with that, I joined the number one IRT team again, and sat, boots on, waiting for a shout.

33. MUSA QALA

Layers of fear creep up my shins like icy tendrils, forcing my muscles into knots. My stomach is taut, my nerves so stretched that every sensation washing over me is like feeling it for the first time. The whine of the engines, the shuddering clamour of the helicopter — even as I look across at my opposite man, Eski, his face seems strange and alien. I try to meditate the fear away, dissipate it by throwing it into the wheel of life which is never-ending tears, hoping that my fear forgets where it lives whilst I step outside of my body for a minute or two. Concentrate on your breathing. In and out. Relax. In and out. Slow your breathing down. Relax. In and out.

I talk to myself like you'd calm a shying horse, and the airframe shudders and screams around me whilst I try to find a peaceful thought whilst airborne in the cold Helmand winter.

When you're airborne, the basest instincts that the infantry can usually cling to are gone. The infantry in contact are like shadows, fleeing the sun. Run, hide- crouched behind rocks, behind dykes, in rivers, anywhere and everywhere the infantryman can find cover. We cling to the ground when all else fails, splayed out like fallen cats, willing the soft loam of the earth to keep us safe. But in the air, there is no such luck. We sit, and wait, and that is all. Wait whilst the pilot throws us around at two hundred miles an hour, banking and weaving to the limits of the aircraft's capability. Wait whilst the Taliban on the ground fire at us, try and kill us in a maelstrom of fiery steel. The time draws near. I sit and wait.

The rear gunner, crouched at his M60 gun, doesn't look back. He raises a hand with two fingers held out — the number of minutes until we land. A message comes, ear to mouth, down the line. The Danish EOD man, to my left, taps my arm. I take my earplug nearest to him out and lean toward him so that his lips nearly brush my ear.

'Six hundred!' he screams. I can barely hear him over the din. 'South!' he screams.

The scenery out of glass-less portholes has changed from empty desert to grey stone-washed wadis and the hint of hardy bushes. Now we are flying over compounds, so low that I can see the hinges on the exterior doors, the bark on the few trees, the soot on the bread chimneys.

'Enemy position!' he screams.

The ground dips and tips as the pilot swoops us in, making the vast bulk of our Chinook a harder target to hit. I raise my thumb to show that I have understood, and the Dane turns away from me again. There is no-one for me to pass the message on to; I sit at the tail-end of the Chinook. We are arranged in two rows, backs to the skin of the airframe, with only the loading ramp to my right. Eski, opposite me, and I will be the first off the ramp when we touch down in just over a minute. Eski because he is the team commander, me because I am a machine gunner. I snap my goggles down over my eyes to protect them against the dust-storm that will be raised when we land.

This is it — the engines' roar takes on a new pitch as the pilot tries to fight physics to slow us and drop us into the landing site. We wheel over a compound so low that it swings and fills the box of visible sky beyond the ramp. We drop suddenly and touch down with a judder in a field a few yards past the compound. Dead poppy stems whip like a frenzy against my face and hands, stirred into semi-life by the downdraught. The rear gunner remains crouched at his gun, and I rush past him. The ramp is not yet fully lowered, and my feet taste the air as I jump out, landing in a crouch. It is nearly 10am, so a few points right of the line of shadow must be south. I run out into the de-cropped field, the tart, crisp mud-hardened ground unyielding beneath my feet. I am master again of my own scroll, feebly tugging at the thread of my life whilst fate weaves around me, and grateful for the illusion of control.

I run into a fire position in the open field, dropping to my knees then hitting the ground with my belly and armour crunching against the hardened mud cracks. The rest of the protection team fan out the same way, each man marking by eye and owning a portion of the landscape. Ahead of me, facing back along the line of the tail, roughly south, a dirty compound leers out of the ground a quick dash away, and stacked up against the near side is a section of men. They are Gurkhas, grim and weary but spurred on, over-revved by adrenaline.

I shift position to focus on the right, taking the western edge of their compound as my left of arc. My heart pounds, my dry throat sticks to itself as I suck air from the short dash to my position. I'm in the open, fifty metres away from the helicopter, but protected from the enemy to the south by the compound walls. Away to the west, the field opens up, leading to more compounds. I see friendly troops forming a perimeter too, around their compounds, kneeling on corners or prone along the wall, waiting for the fight to continue.

Adrenaline courses through me. The excitement of having dropped in this close to an enemy position and be holding ground with troops during a contact mingles with fear, and I'm scanning the ground ahead of me, desperately scouring the landscape for any sign of Taliban. My weapon is cocked, and my heart is in my mouth.

If the Chinook started taking enemy fire, there'll be no doubt that we'll stay on the ground — as soon as the wounded touch the ramp the helicopter would break for home, leaving us to patrol home with the Gurkhas. Whilst I scan my arc ahead, careful not to point Bella in the direction of any friendly troops, I plan in my mind's eye my actions. If mortars land, I am to stay put watching the helicopter leave, then I will tie-in with the Gurkha patrol. If we are contacted by small arms from my arc ahead, I will return fire to supress the enemy, give target indication to my team, move up to better cover whilst they provide fire, then lay down as much fire as Bella can handle until the Gurkhas take the enemy position. Over my gunsight, my eyes scan the ground and my finger rests inside the trigger guard, ready for action.

My breath is regained after my short dash, and now the business of our journey emerges from the compound ahead. Two groups of soldiers are approaching the helicopter, each with a casualty in their midst, stumbling over furrows and bowing their heads against the backwash. As they pass, I faintly hear voices mixing into the cacophony of the rotor-power. Blood has discoloured the side of one of the wounded, and I catch sight of a shock of dark red cloth and a pallid face as they move beyond my sight toward the Chinook. I glance left and right at my fellow soldiers in the protection team, to see if we're being called in yet. The Danish officer to my right has already leapt to his feet and is dashing towards me, doubled over. I give him a thumbs up and prepare to move, relief welling up in my throat like a shameful tear that we'll be riding home today, rather than fighting our way back to a FOB with the Gurkhas. As I dash back to the gangway to board the Chinook, we slow and funnel, and it becomes a mess of bodies. In his haste to leave, the rear gunner has called in the protection team before the stretcher party has left, and we collide and push and surge in and out.

The wounded men are lying on the floor of the Chinook, surrounded by medics and their off-cast accessories. The rear gunner is still screaming 'Get off, get off!' to one lad who found himself at the back of the queue to return to the fight. We plonk down at the sides of the airframe willy-nilly, squeezing in around the wounded, the rear gunner raises a hand to cup around his headset microphone, and the ground pulls away and tilts, as we lift and jink and power away.

I take my eyes off the casualty and look back along the flight line. We've barely levelled out, the rear gunner squats at his M60, the ground rushes away thirty metres below, I see the desert and compounds punctuated with greenery slipping away behind us, and I see a pair of men in dark dish-dash standing on the near side of a compound, holding tubes by their sides. The rear gunner must have seen them to the same moment because he opens fire immediately. The gun barks into life — a 'braap' stutter, then the rear gunner shifts slightly and lets off another burst. There's a puff of dust as bullets churn up the ground, flesh and bone. There's a misting of blood and the first man drops to the ground like a puppet with cut strings. There's a white streak along the ground from the second man, who fires his RPG as the bullets hit him too. Then we bank sharply, and they're lost to sight as a hillcrest passes, and we contour lower.

Back along the flight line, out of sight, lie two dead or dying Taliban, the glory of their martyrdom fading slowly, along with the remaining vestments of life. The blood in their bodies, the warmth of their skin, finally fading, then gone. I can't believe what I've seen, the surreal voyeurism of watching as a spectator whilst men die will grip me later that night. The Royal Marine signaller draws his thumb across his throat, then grins and give me a thumbs up. I look across at the rear gunner, kneeling now amongst the empty brass cases as if they were rose petals, scattered on his head and hands in celebration of his triumph.

◊ ◊ ◊ ◊ ◊

Minutes are stretched out, and the medics fight to keep the casualties alive on the flight back. Two British soldiers have been hit with bullets, and lie flat on their backs, leaking blood and oozing life. The first casualty is further up the helicopter, closer to the nose, and the activity around him goes un-noticed, but it is the man at my feet who holds my attention. The dirt and sweat mixes with aviation fuel in my nostrils as I watch.

A female medic, 20 or so, looking innocent and blonde, unwraps a dressing on his side and re-applies a fresh dressing, showing a ragged hole in the soldier's side when she pulls the used bandage away. The casualty's eyes are open, but keep closing, every time the medic says something to him, he opens them, but then they slowly slide closed again. It feels like a macabre intrusion, this man lying on the deck between two rows of spectators with his injuries and life on show for us. Whilst the medic works, we watch.

◊ ◊ ◊ ◊ ◊

The helicopter jerks and lifts suddenly, and g-force strains at my hands holding my gun, dragging her down as we climb high in the morning sky, light shafts dancing through the portholes. We must be leap-frogging an anti-aircraft threat, we've been told that Marjah and Babaji have ZPU Anti-Aircraft weapons, and there are also rumoured to be Stinger missiles stashed and cached somewhere between Lashkar Gah and Gereshk. If we're lifting over Gereshk, or the towns around Gereshk, then we should be about five minutes from home, and landing at Bastion.

The casualty escapes my attention for a minute, and I peer back along the flightpath, seeing the beautiful tapestry of the landscape below, a patchwork of brown and green fields, orange compounds and scattered trees. It would be easy to get lost in the beauty of this country, and forget that the Pashtun villager and the tribesman of the Taliban were bent on driving us out, and killing as many of us as he can.

◊ ◊ ◊ ◊ ◊

Now that we are higher up, the chill begins to bite my fingers. The tableau beneath us slips further away as we pass Gereshk, the engine noise lessens slightly, and the helicopter begins to descend. Within a minute, the rear gunner waves a hand for attention, then gives us the 'five minutes' signal. I check my safety catch, a habit so automatic that I don't even realise that I'm doing it. The medic at my feet has evidently done all that she can, and kneels by the casualty, writing notes on a piece of fablon.

In another minute or so, we pass the pyramidal peak on our starboard side, the mountain peak that I use as a north marker when breaking down the ground of our AO on patrols. The antennae of FOB Juno are all that's visible of our tiny patch of ground on these hills, but in another few seconds the plain of Dasht-e Margo is beneath us, and it's only a short flight home. Now we're back over familiar country, passing Highway One, and now every gulley, track and dune that I see is reassuringly familiar.

We lift and tilt to come into the wind and begin the landing, and below us is now Bastion, a sea of shipping containers, tents, sangars and work-yards. I pull my goggles down over my eyes, and as we slow and hover and drop the dust-storm kicked up billows. Amidst the noise and dust, I feel wheels bouncing down.

The rear gunner gives us a thumbs up, we are clear to deplane, and men grab stretchers and hurry out of the helicopter and down the tail ramp. The Danish officer and I are carrying the man who was at my feet, and we struggle across the shingle and fist-sized stones of the HLS towards an ambulance fifty metres away. The ambulance crew are on their feet as we struggle up to the ambulance and load the stretcher into the back. Doors slam, blue lights flash, and the wagon drives my casualty across the hospital. The second man is loaded onto a second ambulance, as I run doubled-over back to the helicopter. The rear gunner clears us to emplane, I jump on, crunch across the rose-petal empty bullet cases and take my place. A few seconds after the last man hops on we lift again, wheeling over the Bastion sky to the flight line, on our way back to the IRT tent.

34. THE SHAVING BOWL

I stand alone in the wash block, head bowed, staring into the shaving bowl. Grief has come, the cracks in the dike have given way at last and a flood of sorrow breaks over me. He is gone. Dead. He will never stand at the alter with his fiancé, never see the pride on his parents' faces when he hands them their grandchild. We will never again raise the rafters with laughter together, never wake on exercise to his cheerful Devonian drawl, and share hardships together as comrades. Tears pour down my face, and my body shakes silently.

We were born days apart, though I never met him until I became a Rifleman. Our lives walked the same path though. Whenever I think back to my own schooldays, there is Chris, the same age, smiling up at the camera in my mind. Whenever I think into the past, anytime, I see him: a son, a brother, a friend, as a child, a man, a soldier. And now a memory.

His photo on the evening news, like all the others, has pricked the nation's hearts for a few moments. 'Those poor boys,' they will say, then they will go back to their lives and forget.

I can see the future, from this lonely corner of Helmand.

When I walk the road of life long after this deployment is over, it will be marked by his memory. Every milestone will ache with his absence, every triumph and joy will be lessened.

My heart is broken. I pick up the shards and knit them together with hatred, and violence. The Taliban who did this, down in Garmsir, are far beyond my reach. Perhaps they are already dead. Or, more likely, we will never know who built the IED that killed him, who buried it, who watched his patrol heading for death and celebrated the explosion. But life pays for life. It doesn't matter which Taliban to me, they are all guilty of his murder. They owe, and they must pay. Vengeance will be mine. I will kill, I swear it. I raise my bloodshot eyes to my reflection, and a whisper escapes my lips.

'I swear it.'

35. MAIL-CALL

I am back in Wyvern lines as cold mizzle clouds the air, and a shipment of mail has arrived from home. Our taciturn Company Quarter Master Serjeant makes his way through North Hill, dropping off letters and boxes at each tent with a grunt. I riffle through my tent's allocation, and with surprise find my name staring back at me. The parcel is a battered shoebox, the lid stuck down with heavy tape, and the hand-inked lettering around my name has a familiar flourish to the script. I read the return address. It's from Maggie. Maggie was one of my closest friends from my insurance sales days. I sit down on my bunk and open the box, hidden from prying eyes. A letter lies closed on top of a hoard. Chocolate and sweets, biscuits and Jaffa cakes. I save the best until last, the letter, and pick out a bottle of fruit juice, seal broken and re-sealed. This can only mean one thing — smuggled booze.

I hold the letter and close my eyes. For a moment I feel like a civilian again, full of the excitement of Friday night, the anticipation of drinking and laughing with friends; all of us young, underpaid, the overeducated middle class, stuck in hum-drum jobs and living for the weekend. I remember how we used to meet in our industrial-gothic drinking den, a vision in blue neon. We would clock off at different times but would all meet, drink, talk and throng. This was the Indian Summer of my youth, nearly mid-20s and devil-may-care, two fingers to the world on warm summer nights, swilling cheap lager, surrounded by friends, talking of the future whilst we waited for our lives to bring us all our dreams.

Now the Queen's uniform is poorly draped over my frame, I have £16,000 a year and bags under my eyes. My fingers shake when I smoke after IRT, and my washboard stomach has faded away. What do I have now? What have I traded my Friday nights for? Sullen conversation with my girlfriend once a week on a satellite phone, and half-asleep pulling on my helmet during night-time rocket attacks.

I open the letter and read the note, written in purple ink. Maggie is well. Ryan and Anca send their best. She is sorry it's taken her so long to put together a care package, but she had to wait until she got paid at the end of the month. She hopes I enjoy the refreshing fruit juice (wink). She heard about Chris, the news said a Rifleman from Plymouth had been killed and she was in a state, thinking it was me. But it wasn't me, so that was alright.

I stop reading. Oh Maggie, it was not alright. Nothing could be further from alright. No matter what else happens in the world, Chris is gone. He is a memory, a headstone, medals in a drawer and a maudlin toast once a year from a platoon that, by dribs and drabs, new faces and newer, will make their way in a world that moves further away from the one that we shared with him. I finish the letter in a sour mood and hide my smuggled whisky in a sock in a boot in a bag under my cot bed, and forget about it.

◊ ◊ ◊ ◊ ◊

Jacobs sticks his head into my cubbyhole. 'Addy, a bunch of us are going to the EFI, you want in?'

We walk over along the dusty road, US armour

thundering past with full beam lights on. We smoke roll ups around the picnic tables, lit up in orange florescence. My hands are steady, but there's a sad detachment in the pit of my stomach. I feel like there is a veil between my comrades and I, and the chatter passes me by as if I were someplace else.

36. BOGGED IN BY HIGHWAY ONE

The desert is quiet, nightfall came and took the light hours ago. It is moonless, thick clouds drawn overhead blot out even the most tenacious stars. Parcels of invisible condensation blow out softly from chilled noses and cracked lips. There are six men from my company on night patrol, and I one of them. Night patrol in Helmand. We edge our way, wheels creaking slowly over the dips, runnels, and hills of the central wadi high ground. On a night so dark as this, that your eyes roll weakly, vainly trying to pick up peripheral light, and every nerve is strained from listening for signs of life stirring in the hamlets of the wadi, the time drags like nothing else.

I am disorientated, only the twin glows of Bastion and Nad Ali, west and south, showing the compass direction, but the little hills and spurs and re-entrants of day's familiarity, are swallowed up by the blackness. Tracer fire spits into the sky from time to time down in Nad Ali. Our drivers have green-glow faces from night vision goggles clamped to their heads, but we do not have enough to go around and the top covers have to make do with wide-eyes straining into the night. We roll on, black light headlights and occasional snatches of familiarity as I spot a compound

157

silhouette that orients my internal map for a moment or two. We roll forward, creeping and creaking, until — we stop.

What's happened? I cock my GPMG and ready myself. The radio chatters away, and I understand. Whilst we are making our way up the slopes of the eastern wadi, the lead vehicle has driven over a shallow ledge and grounded the belly, front wheels hanging inches off the floor. There's nothing for it but to dig ourselves out with pickaxes and shovels, breaking up the ground until the front wheels touch down and we can move again.

The patrol commander tells us to go light. I can hardly believe my ears. Go light? Turn on our yellow headlights to illuminate the beached vehicle? When we are only two vehicles in total! He wants the men to see what they're doing whilst I provide top cover. Orders are orders, and within minutes, we are spilling yellow light into the darkness. We must be visible for miles around, I think, and I grit my teeth and ready myself for contact.

The minutes drag. Dogs bray their hoarse, coughing barks down in the nearest village, and I itch to move. I have a pricking feeling in the pit of my stomach, and the hair on the back of my neck is raised. I feel that we are being watched, and I don't like it one bit. The thudding bite of the picks slows as the men tire, but the commander urges them on. They down tools for a second, and an engine note builds as the WMIK driver tries to move off, but they're a little short. Another minute of digging, and we should be safe. In the distance, on Highway One, headlights moving by slow down as they pass the Russian checkpoint near Catford. We try again, and the front vehicle rocks back and forward a few times, until the belly plates slide over the ledge and we start moving off again. We go dark, and I can feel my hands shake from more than the cold underneath my gloves. The lights on Highway One move again, picking up speed and hurtling towards Gereshk. We move on, and I want to close my eyes and lose myself in the desert, tiny and safe, the only man alive in this world.

37. TALIBAN RECCE PATROL

We are out in the wadi, and we have a pair of them. Taliban for sure. Unarmed, yes — they are reconnoitring instead of fighting, but they are Taliban. I sight my GMPG on the motorbikes thirty metres away. I have my range slider set to two hundred metres and aim low so the recoil will pull the weapon up, one short burst per man. The weapon is cocked but I re-cock it to make sure the working parts are fully to the rear and click the safety off with the side of my thumb. The WMIK is alongside my Vector, with the vehicle commander shouting commands at the Taliban. The interpreter is shouting alongside him, trying to make his Pashto heard, and one of the Taliban is calling back and gesturing with his arm. No-one has seen me re-cock my weapon.

Suicide bombers, I think. I'll say they were suicide bombers. That I thought they were suicide bombers, I correct myself. It was my honest belief that life was in danger. Warning shot? I'll shout 'warning shot' then start shooting. No-one can say I didn't fire a warning; it'll end up in chaos and I can just claim that my warning shots and actual shots were close together.

I settle the stock of the weapon firm into my shoulder

and tense up in anticipation of the recoil. First pressure on the trigger as I rehearse my actions. I will kill the man on the left first, but with a short burst, then I will shift aim quickly to the man on the right. White-hot with hatred, anger and adrenaline, I feel lightheaded. This is actually it. I am going to murder two unarmed enemy in revenge for Chris.

Then, over the radio and directly into my ear, 'Addy, all-round defence mate, Ngabo's got these covered.' The driver of the WMIK has looked about and seen me in firing position. I blow my cheeks out with a ragged breath, and spin 180-degrees, and suddenly my hatred and anger have given way to bone-weary sadness at what I have become. The Taliban are unarmed, and we have no reason to arrest them, so we must let them go. Those are the rules.

◊ ◊ ◊ ◊ ◊

That night, by red torchlight in the section tent, I get drunk on Maggie's whisky. I share a little with Jacobs, but I have nearly finished the bottle by the time I pass it over.

'Jacobs,' I tell him, 'I nearly had a pair of them today.'

He looks up, grinning like a maniac. 'Go on,' he urges, bloodthirsty and eager to hear the details.

I start to explain, and I'm going to tell him everything. He interrupts me when I tell him there were two of them, old men with white beards, on a motorbike apiece, scouting around the previous night's rocket attack launch site.

'Taliban,' he pronounces. 'Definitely Taliban. Mate, you should have brassed them up.'

I tell him about being at first pressure, but then getting spotted — saved — by the vehicle commander of the WMIK.

Jacobs is having none of it. 'Screw him and screw you, you pussied out big time. You just lost your bottle, so what if anyone saw you? I'd have shot them. Both of them. You pussied out. This is war. And I'm going to get some kills. I thought you were cool, Addy. Turns out you're just another REMF.'

This is too much. I am bursting with anger at his callous judgement. 'Screw you, Jacobs.'

He mimics me with a sneer. 'Screw you Jacobs, you weren't there, man.' Then he laughs again. I snatch back the remainder of my bottle of whisky and drink it in my sleeping bag in the dark.

◊ ◊ ◊ ◊ ◊

The next day I am on vehicle patrols again with 2 Platoon's other multiple. I wake with a throbbing head at 0500 and lie there in a daze staring at the canvas roof over my head. I drag myself out of bed and mope to the wash block, to blow out toothpaste bubbles under bloodshot eyes. My gear weighs heavy as I lug and struggle my gun, ammo, armour, helmet and daysack, and head over to the vehicles, tired and heavy, and on to the new day.

The days are almost on the turn, and for the brief spells when the cold wind yields to the yellow light of a struggling springtime sun, there is even a little warmth in the air. Tinges of the new year have coloured our days and nights, and as the spring creeps in we roll out of camp in a thunder of dust. Today we have a pair of Vixens to patrol in. We make our way through the gateway, passing guards, bunkers and sangars, then turn for south as we break off the main roadway. The ranges are quiet and still, and we lose ourselves from sight in a sea of rolling stone dunes as we pitch and toss our way down the western desert. Small farmsteads rise into sight to our sides as the dunes open out, the mud brick compounds of the Pashtun, each with a small acreage of hand-tilled rough soil waiting for the poppies to come. Then, as quickly as we spot them, they are gone again, as more rolling dunes sweep us away with the spinning of our wheels. I stand in the rear of the rear vehicle, feet splayed and balanced on two benches, my body pokes through the sunroof-style top cover hatch and I lay my chest flat to the roof to keep a low profile. With an oiled and cocked gun to my shoulder, I watch back along our path and cover the 180-degree rear arc.

The west is quieter than the remainder of our AO. In the north, Highway One brings convoys, travellers, locals and out-of-area Afghans, passing through to Gereshk, and the north–south central wadi serves for those passing through to Nad Ali, turning north for Kajaki or Sangin. When we patrol the roads and trails I am always on the lookout for suicide bombers, for fighters travelling without weapons, for IEDS and ambush points, for everything and anything that could kill us before we even know something is out of place. In the east, the farms and compounds tightly cluster on the high ground, getting denser and denser as you go until you find the start of the sprawl from Gereshk. And south — I know nothing in the pit of my stomach like the feeling I get whenever we turn south for Nad Ali — six men in two vehicles, encroaching on the Taliban's homeland and heartland one Land Rover at a time; threading our way between compounds and villages, through wet fields and irrigation trenches and ditches until home is one long, long fight through hostile towns that we can never make if we come into a heavy contact with well organised fighters.

Last time the Rifle Regiment supplied troops for this patrol was winter 2006 on Herrick 5, and a whole platoon got hit by the canal in a co-ordinated ambush. The Taliban spotted the platoon coming and threw everything they had at them. An RPG ambush opened the contact, and in the frantic close-quarter battle a Land Rover got destroyed whilst the platoon fought their way out back the way they came, and Eski had to run back through enemy fire to the exposed vehicle shell to destroy the EWDs with a phosphorous grenade. South — the hornets' nest — and the gnawing fear of just two vehicles and six men re-visiting Nad Ali outskirts is a bitter tonic, when a whole platoon barely escaped only two years ago.

West though, once you have swept past the high ground farmers and picked up the western wadi, is sparsely populated, shielded from view by the wadi walls, yet with good all-round visibility. I like the west, as instead of taking us amongst villages, there is only one village of nomads encamped around an old well and a lone tree. They are our friends, for as long as we are there and sharing our water. The Taliban do not bother them, they don't farm poppies and have no money to extort and simply move to another camp in another area if there was to be any hassle. Today is a lazy day, as we are going to lease some more hearts and minds from the village headman with a crate of water and some old clothes collected from home and intended for their children.

As we patrol out westerly in our vehicles, the commander briefs us on the personal radio, 'Heading for Blue Seventeen, overwatch A1.' We are making our way, slowly, back to the main highway running west-east, where we will sit and watch the traffic, brew tea in mess tins and slowly run down the clock on another day in Afghanistan.

38. DRUNK ON DUTY

The memorial service is done, the coffin has been loaded aboard a transport plane, and the Bloody Eleventh hold a wake for Chris that night in my tent, pooling our meagre stashes of whisky and defying all known whisky-drinking convention by pouring everything we have into one oversized litre mug. We sit in a circle in the dim light, slowly passing the mug about our circle from hand to hand, each man cradling it in his turn whilst we tell stories about Chris. I hear about his laughter, his love of life, his heart, his humour, his warmth. I hear about all the things now gone from this world, and the world has scarcely noticed.

My turn comes around. I have not been in the platoon as long as the rest of them, most of my stories are from pre-deployment training. I tell an old one, not a funny old yarn that will have our sides aching, but something that goes towards reminding the Bloody Eleventh of one facet of this gem called a human life. One brief, glinting moment that I saw part of the man and they did not, just as they have told me of the same things they had seen. I begin.

It was Tuesday, late, and TA training had already given way to the weekly drinking session in the platoon bar. I had arrived on parade earlier that day with my hair touching my collar, and Serjeant P, a grim stickler who seemed to hate recruits with a disdain bordering on obsessive, had noticed at once. My punishment was to sweep out the locker rooms, which were littered with encrusted mud after a fitness training session has seen us sprinting up and down Plymouth Citadel's earthen ramparts. Now, alone after training, I stooped and swept and swept and stooped, whilst my comrades made merry. Until, that is, the door opened, and Chris came in. With a grin, he stepped forward and took the broom from me. Still a Corporal at this stage, waiting his promotion to Serjeant, we were at the mercy of his rank. And what did he do with this power? With the power of punishment in his hand, he decided to show a kindness that I had no right to expect — and took my punishment for me, shooing me away to the bar as he cleaned up after us all. Half an hour later he joined us there, with not a word passing his lips to embarrass me or to show anyone what he had done.

I break off, and take my allotted glug of whisky, passing the mug to my left. The stories move on, and my tale of the generosity, the decency, the sheer heart of this man has passed by, superseded by the side-aching stories that Chris left behind him as he travelled to the end of the earth and the end of his short life. He will not grow old, as we who are left grow old. The cup empties, the stories are running dry and our heads are swimming with booze. Finally, reluctantly, we take our leave of each other and abruptly the wake is at an end. We retire to our bunks, and the world spins as I lie down, stomach heavy with sadness.

39. IED STRIKE UPPER SANGIN VALLEY

The fire burns low in the blown-apart wreckage, a heap of mangled, crushed metal. We fan out along the embankment, hugging the ground, weapons ready and pulses tightened. The day hangs heavy overhead, grey and stark. Last night's rain still lingers on the clay-heavy soils, and as I look past the wreckage a rainbow-slick of oil which has bled out catches my eye and shimmers atop a pool, whilst I scan the middle ground.

The convoy was hit on this capillary road, snaking past a village somewhere in the Sangin Valley. To my left along the road, the front vehicles have ground to a halt and now bristle with weapons and impotent anger. Directly ahead of me, only twenty metres away, the wreckage of a former Humvee smoulders and burns down, and to my right along the road the tail of the American convoy stretches back towards their FOB or fire base. The roar of the Chinook's engines drowns shouts around me, so I rely on hand signals from Jacobs to let me know what's happening in his arc to my left. I lower my profile on the bank, aware that, if anything kicks off, I am directly between the Chinook and the village across the road, from where the threat of sniper fire is highest. Hunkered down over my gun, I scan the compounds ahead. Past the wreckage there is about a hundred metres of waste ground, empty and barren, just forgotten land collecting dust and turning it through silent industry into clinging mud.

Not a soul stirs in the village ahead. I glance left and right, taking in the ground, the friendly activity, looking out for possible firing points and ranging in my head the distance to each one. I see choke points, areas of extremely high IED threat, and possible markers that might indicate secondary IED points. An ambulance sits to the right of me, still amidst the cacophony of shouting and buzzing engines. A flag flying from a compound ahead flutters, green and weak, like a dying fish, showing the Taliban defiance of our presence. And so, we wait and watch, alone in the crowd of hubbub and din.

A corpse, sheet-covered, emerges under a gang of hands from the ambulance. The stretcher is covered, but an arm hangs out limply from under the sheet, naked and tattered. The American soldiers carrying him to the helicopter stumble under mis-matched paces, then recover and plod on. Jacobs grins in excitement, his wide eyes dancing over the landscape, watching for someone to shoot. I, too, have my weapon cocked and the safety catch off. As they pass by, I register the grief and anger on the faces of his comrades. As the vortex of emotions whirl around me but leave me untouched, I concentrate on searching the landscape ahead for signs of Taliban, ready for contact. How many times have we done this? I feel nothing, looking at the corpse being hauled aboard the helicopter. I have bargained away my compassion for a little while and replaced it with fear and duty.

We've been on the ground for several minutes, and I'm getting impatient. The strength of the convoy is a comfort

— had our patrol of two or three vehicles been caught by this IED, within minutes we'd be overwhelmed by incoming fire. Clearly the Taliban aren't confident of taking on the convoy, perfectly correct guerrilla warfare tactics. Fight when you can win. The threat of a straight stand-up fight, small arms contact is low, but we're far from safe. The threat of a RPG or mortar attack is quite high, so we watch and wait. The longer we're on the ground, the higher the chance of a snap baseplate setting up and lobbing mortar rounds. We've been here a few minutes, so I shout across to Jacobs to sub-divide our arc down,

'Left compound with trees — right hand edge. That's my left of arc.'

He looks across and cups a hand to his ear. I shout again, and he nods and grins, and mimes pulling a trigger repeatedly, then gives me a thumbs up. I grin back, then look over my sights again, wiping the sweat off my palm on my shoulder, then adjusting my hand on the pistol grip. The skeletal vehicle grabs my gaze again, sooty smoke still oozing weakly out, but I force myself to look past it and focus again on the compounds ahead. All we can see of the village are walls facing us, with the accessories of a scratched existence scattered around, irrigation pipes and a pump, a few sheets of wriggly tin, and other magpie treasures. There are no children visible, which is a big sign that we're in a dangerous spot. The locals' reaction to us varies, when they keep their distance or aren't around at all, they either are worried that Taliban will see them talking to us, or know there'll be fighting and want to be far from harm's way.

The stretcher team dashes back from the helicopter, ducked down both from the rotor wash, and to keep their profile lower. They reach the ambulance, and in my peripheral vision I see another stretcher emerging. A gang, perhaps the same as carried the first casualty, stumbles the second casualty behind me and aboard, whilst ahead of me the stucco mud-walled compounds show no sign of the enemy. No-one for Jacobs or I to shoot today. Jacobs jumps us, and seeing him do so, I know that we've been called back to the helicopter. I click Bella's safety catch back on, clamber to my feet, heaving under the bulk of my body armour and weight of my ammunition. I join my comrades, converging in on the short dash back to the helicopter. As always, the power of the rotor wash stops my ears, but even amidst the din I can hear faintly the slamming of armoured doors on the road, and the convoy moves off again.

The engine note of the Chinook rises, the familiar disorientation comes as we lift, tilt and spin for home, weaving our way into the air. The pilot tips the nose down, and we race away. The American soldiers lie head to toe in the gangway and once again we are ghoulish observers in the scene played out before us. In front of us, close enough to see the grime in his pores, a young man with cropped blonde hair, pain and shock across his face, has leg wounds tended to by two medics. His trousers are tattered, his bloody, bootless stumps sticking pale into the air. His comrade, up front, is beyond help. He has an IV-bag running into his left arm, but the medics do no more. His face is obliterated, charred, featureless and misshapen. Most of his uniform is missing, only the remains of his shirt, grey and limp, still cling on to his trunk, stuck in places in watery, bloody clumps. He is naked below the waist, his blackened skin hanging off in tatters like a poorly peeled potato. He must have been caught in the burning wreck, I think, and stare transfixed as we shudder in the air current, bringing two soldiers — one alive, one dead — back to the hospital and eventually home to their families. The adrenaline still tingles in my veins with every heartbeat, but now the familiar buzz is being replaced with a feeling of sickness. I tear my eyes away and try not to look at the burnt corpse in the front of the helicopter, or the face of the solider with no feet who is lying at mine. I thumb my safety catch and close my eyes, putting up a wall between me and the outside world.

The flight back takes longer; we are racing into a headwind, and the helicopter swings back and forth under the rotor disc. After a time, the ashen concrete walls of Bastion pass by the tail ramp, colour returns to the scene through the blue and red shipping containers. The helicopter drops and spirals and flares, and we thump down onto the landing zone outside the hospital. I am on stretcher duty, and I hand Bella to the Royal Marine signaller sitting up the helicopter, kneel down at the canvas stretcher, hand reaching back onto the wooden carry handles, facing down ramp, and wait for the command from the number one to lift.

'Two, one, LIFT!' comes over the roar of the engines, and I haul myself up as evenly as I can, though the heavy plate of the body armour makes this a hard task. When I feel the stretcher is even, I step off, we march down the ramp, then

'Two, one, GO!' from the number one man when his feet are down the ramp, and we break into a slow jog, cushioning the stretcher from bouncing by absorbing the shock in our elbows and lifting between each step. The medic keeps pace beside the stretcher, holding handwritten notes to handover to the ambulance team. We arrive at the ambulance, and load the casualty into ambulance feet first — no, stumps first — and dash back to the Chinook whilst the medic goes through the process of handing over treatment notes, vital signs, and the like. We pass the second stretcher team carrying the corpse. The medic walking alongside holds no notes, just keeps a silver foil sheet over the body with a hand, as the downdraught whips and tries to rip it away.

I take a seat, regain my weapon from the signaller, and check the safety catch. I can stretch my feet out a little further now that the casualties are offloaded, and try and regain a sense of normality. Blood has stained my sleeve from the stretcher carry, and I'll need to wash thoroughly before I settle back into the IRT routine of tea and biscuits, weapon cleaning and cat napping, laundry runs and letter writing. The Chinook heaves into the sky on the way back to flight line, and Big Jimmy is sitting in the stripped Land Rover waiting for us before we have even landed. Kit is hauled, hanging off shoulders and dangling off straps from the crooks of elbows, we help each other up into the back, and speed off the tarmac. Back at the tent now, we relax a little - after a shout we go on the standby watch, and the second team is on immediate notice to move.

'Cup of tea, Addy?' Chalky is on tea duty, probably so he can complain that he did his tea duty in Ireland, and it's someone else's turn. I have a cup of tea, and we debrief the new immediate notice team over hot, sweet tea. 'Good shout then?'

Jacobs tells the details to the tent. He recounts the location near Sangin, the armoured convoy and the green Taliban flag, the US soldiers and the stretcher run. He skips over the injuries, 'They were in pretty bad shape, poor bastards,' then vents his spleen at not having anyone to shoot. I sip my tea and my eyes glaze over, my mind drifting; miles away from my comrades until I fall asleep on my cot bed.

40. OPERATION DIESEL

It's a cold, late winter morning as February is dying. The poppies are nosing their blunt green way through the tough soils. In Garmsir, there's an empty bunk where Chris used to sleep. The Rifle Regiment is losing more men, and we who knew the dead struggle on, guiltily remembering our friends in glimpses through our everyday lives, the memory of a joke or a kind word. We struggle on, our thoughts heavy with unspoken loss. But our grief cannot hold back the dawn, and the breaking day brings new work and fresh dangers.

The dawning sun shows red through the night's heavy cloud, and Bastion sighs into life. Morning prayers are over, the minarets far away across the wadi and down in Nad Ali once again empty. Spewed to the fields, the Pashtun farmers heave picks and hoes to their bony shoulders and toil on. But the day's work has begun in earnest for us, too. It isn't long before the light snaking through the IRT tent flaps goads the first of us into rising. I volunteer for tea duty and three new faces appear through the tent flap as I'm busying myself with the tea, to relieve Bazza, Jacobs and Chalky. New faces find their bunks and settle into the 'off' shift, and I finish handing around Styrofoam cups of tea to each man in turn. I flop back on my cot bed in the corner whilst the radio chatters in the background, and clean Bella, more to give myself something to do than for any real need. I'm ready to go with the first flight today though, so I wipe oil out of her guts with a rag, blow sand and grit from the magazine housing, and dash around the muzzle with a paintbrush.

Five minutes later, maybe less, and the radio crackles.

'IRT this is ops.'

The now-familiar adrenaline rush races through me like a drug, and I grab my gear and haul myself into the back of the stripped-down Land Rover. Within minutes we are at the flight line, and our helicopter is already turning and burning, rotors spinning, engines high, waiting for the troops to file in and fill the helicopter before we race to the contact. We dash over at a half crouch with a thumbs up from the rear gunner, then up the ramp and find a seat on the canvas, and with that we lift and turn and are away.

Minutes drag by. I look out of the porthole opposite for a clue where we are headed. North somewhere, north east, I think, as we are flying over increasingly rugged terrain. The rocky hills rise up in the space of a minute or two and become mountainous, and we weave and bob, shaking and correcting our way through narrow mountain passes, whilst the rocky grey and brown peaks loom around us. The Chinook roars through the valleys, skirting so close to the mountainsides on either side of us that I close my eyes and hold my breath on one banking, swooping turn; clutching tight to the frame of our canvas bench, and to Bella. Operation Diesel, an air assault from Chinook helicopters, is going on today somewhere in the upper Sangin valley. The troops have been staged through Bastion in the last few days and now they're on the ground, moving into place or in contact already. We must be going towards Sangin.

The rear gunner has a miniature whiteboard pinned to the airframe at the back of the Chinook, by his control panel. We have cleared the mountain passes now, and drop down towards Sangin valley floor. As we do so the rear gunner gets to his feet, pulls a marker pen from his smock and begins to write. Boundary trees and scattered compounds squat on the tapestry plains around us, nestled in the green zone, far away from our law and control. The rear gunner scribbles away. As I concentrate on the whiteboard, there is a sudden bang, and white smoke explodes from the tail, raining orange sparks, and at the same time we bank sharply and skitter across the sky, furiously changing direction and swinging like a pendulum below the rotors. I feel sick, but it is only the emergency flares. We haven't been hit, but there's ground-fire incoming already. The flares deploy again with another loud rapport, and the pilot swings up around in the air, taking evasive action to make us harder to hit. At the bang, the rear gunner had jumped back to his M60, but now he stands again and resumes writing at the whiteboard. I look again, and my heart pounds harder when I see what he has written.

LZ in contact. HMG IDF SA. Wait AH bang.

Translated, this means that the landing zone is under attack by heavy machine guns, mortars, and small arms, so we are waiting for an Apache gunship's attack run before landing.

We bank and wheel, still descending, and the Chinook screams in the air, flailing and diving. My heart races, my throat is parched, and I look around, super-alert, seeing the ground, now the sky, now the ground again through the porthole in front of me. I check Bella, nervously thumbing the safety catch. Flares pop out again as the ground fire increases. The pilot takes us level, and we thump down, tail first, at such speed that the wheels dig a gouge twenty metres long before the nose touches down.

The wheels are barely down as we jump out, then my feet pound on the ground, I fight my way through settling dust, and we fan out to our fire positions. I hear the familiar old click-clack as I cock Bella, then thumb the safety catch on. I stop, drop to the ground, and deploy my machinegun ready to fire, bipod down, checking Litch and the Dane fifty metres either side of me, and take in my arc. I'm out on the left flank of the landing zone and the Chinook.

The first thing I see is an expanse of empty ground, the dusty ochre of bare earth churned up by vehicle tracks. Away ahead of me is a cluster of fighting vehicles: light Jackals and a few WMIKs, where it looks like Commando Brigade Reconnaissance Force have been hit. In the shadows of their lightly armoured Jackal fighting vehicles cluster Royal Marine troops, grizzled and dusty. One Jackal is off to a flank, the remainder are ahead of me. Ashen faces mark the men holding the casualty as they move in my peripheral vision, an angry, dusty gang hauling their stricken friend towards the helicopter. A soldier tries to sit up on the stretcher, and pain sparks across his face as his shifts his weight. Ahead of me, where the valley we have flown from joins another, Brigade Reconnaissance Force troops run between vehicles, carrying ammo boxes. Beyond the vehicles the valley snakes away into the distance, with mud compounds and vivid green treelines showing sparks of life amidst the barren nothingness. In the air further away, the Apache hangs in the air for a second, changing direction, training his 30mm cannon on something further down the valley. Then the gunship moves up and circles in a vast arc like an angry hornet, keeping the Taliban in cover whilst we get the injured man out of contact.

I scan the ground of my arc again, seeing only empty fields away south, from where we came, a few compounds in the distance, but no movement. The day is bright and crisp, and on the plain to my left, stretching back into the distance and Bastion, an expanse of valley, which curves away in front of me and into the west. The hillside slopes of the valley in front of me are in shadow at the base, and further up the valley I see a wisp of smoke, clearing faintly in the cold morning air, from where the Apache just destroyed an enemy position. I bite the inside of my cheek as I watch my arc. The Taliban are still out there, up the valley, and the Commandos will fight through their positions when our Chinook lifts off, leaving death and destruction behind them. Unlike Jacobs, I have stopped feeding my hatred, and my desire to kill has withered to die amidst the blood of the IRT flights, replaced by numbness.

The stretcher moves beyond my vision, and we'll be airborne again soon. I watch my arc as the casualty is hefted aboard the helicopter behind me, and then a Danish officer breaks his position and runs over to me. I leap up, stow the legs on Bella, and run back to the Chinook. Looking back, I see the casualty's mates loading themselves into a wagon to return to the fight up the valley. I leap aboard the ramp and take my position on the seats against the fuselage.

This is the worst part. Taking off under fire is worse than landing under fire. I think back to that day in Musa Qala, the Taliban fighters dying in a wall of bullets, and RPGs flying through the air at us. The rotors whirl and roar, the casualty is flat on his back on the stretcher on the floor in front of us, drifting in and out of consciousness whilst paramedics kneel around, expertly, furiously working their craft. The din rushes in and we lift like from a catapult, surging through the air, more flares deploy as we spin towards home and weave at low level and high speed away from the HLS.

I look across at Litch. He's grinning broadly and tried to mouth something to me. Angry, I look away. It doesn't seem right to laugh and joke when there's an injured man in front of us. The frenzy around the casualty dies down, and as we judder in the air, racing back to Bastion, my eyes are drawn to the blood on the floor of the Chinook. A dark stream has run from the stretcher at my feet, and I stare at the blood, wondering if my own blood will seem so dark.

That night I'm relieved of IRT duty, to be back on

patrols at 0530. I pack my ammunition and warm clothing, haul my armour and gun over my shoulder, and trail back to Wyvern Lines with Vince and Conlay. A letter is waiting for me from Charlotte. As I sit reading, the camp tannoy splutters and crackles into life — 'All Callsigns. Op minimise is now in effect. I say again Op minimise is now in effect. End of message. End of broadcast.'

41. DANISH ARMOUR

The late winter air is still wet, and the stones of the desert shine like stars with the first rays of light. The freeze came quickly, blowing off the mountains to the north and wrapping our coats tighter around our shoulders. I am in an airfield sanger, and dawn is breaking. I have spent the last three hours watching the wadi for movement. It is a new moon, which is the best time to attack under cover of night, when the cold bites, and sentries are off guard. Open to the air on four sides, the top floor bunker sucks the warmth from us overnight, and I come off sentry to find the water frozen fast in my bottle. My fingers are stiff inside my gloves, but I have no time to warm up; during the morning radio checks, I was told to report to the work-yard to go out on patrol. I pass the interpreters' tent on my way through company lines, and Aziz and Jamshed are already up, fresh from prayer and sitting on their body armour, wrapped up in blankets and smoking thin cigars, waiting for a platoon to call for them. I have been tasked to bring an interpreter with me, so I pick Jamshed, and we walk together to find our vehicles.

The Vector is mine today, and Jamshed waits until I have loaded up with batteries and water, ammunition and the

GPMG, before he climbs in and sits inside. I clip my helmet on, tighten my ammo straps, and thrust my body and shoulders through the top cover hatch and take my place at the gun. We are lead vehicle, so I spin the gun to face our front, plant my legs wide, bend my knees ready for the ride ahead and call over the radio, 'Top cover ready.'

Our patrol brief was simple: escort a Danish armoured unit to the north of our AO, and we set off in column, Vector in front, a pair of Danish APCs, a Danish Leopard tank, then a WMIK in the rear. We are more heavily armed and armoured than I have ever patrolled before, and the usual pre-patrol knot in my stomach is gone.

◊ ◊ ◊ ◊ ◊

We know the AO well by now, the choke points and the runnels, the low ground and the high ground. We head north west, handrailing Highway One at a wary distance, then we spin north and the patrol commander checks his map. We cross the concrete road, and the patrol commander marks the spot on his map with a sticky dot; no patrols will cross here again. We have a grid square close to the mountains of FOB Juno as our target, where a pressure plate IED has been identified by an intelligence agent working for us. The Danish ATO are going to try and recover it, and learn as much as they can about this bomb-maker's habits — his tools and techniques, his safety switches and his tamper switches, his main charge and his ignition charge. They will, if they can, learn where the deadly shrapnel that coats his bomb came from — is it sheet steel cut with tin snips from Iranian shipyards, Pakistani screws and iron nails, or is it made from hammered flat British and ISAF link, the metal clips that hold belts of ammunition together then the Taliban recycle to use against us.

There are two philosophies at war here: engineering and intelligence. Engineers don't care who made it or where it came from, they want it neutralised in the safest way, which means controlled detonation. Intelligencers want to know who the bomb makers are, where their components are made and who handles them, and where they are assembled. That means recovering intact, disassembling, and analysing. Enough pieces of the puzzle will end with a Reaper UAV fitted with hellfire missiles, circling the night sky and piloted from Kandahar, and the bomb maker will be obliterated on his way to or from a meeting. Clipped tones over the radio will report the devastation; with a successful mission stencil to be painted on the drone, and celebration for the pilots and Reaper team.

We stop short of our objective, and my patrol sets up defences to let the Danish EOD team work. We have a rock outcrop as partial cover, but good visibility to the south, and my vehicle covers a narrow arc, watching the empty desert through weapon sights. Minutes, then hours pass as we watch and wait.

There is no question that we will ask the Danes how long it will be. No matter the rank, no matter the urgency, no matter if rounds are flying — no-one rushes the EOD team. It takes as long as it takes. The Russians thirty years ago had a saying: a sapper only makes one mistake. The Danes have recently lost a number of their men wounded in an explosion, and we have new faces riding with us on the IRT, a new Danish EOD team. They will not make a mistake today.

The morning, promising a milder day, retreats as the cold rolls off the mountains again. I change the radio batteries and grab half an hour's rest in the Vector whilst Ngabo takes post at the GPMG. Chalky pours me tea from his thermos, and I break open a bar of chocolate from the rations. The Afghans have a custom: no matter how little you have to eat, you must offer to share it, even with a total stranger. I break the chocolate in two and offer to Jamshed. 'Melmastia,' I explain, the Pashto word for their custom of sharing, and he smiles and accepts. I drink the tea with a slurp, and feel the hot liquid warm my belly and chase the chill from my fingers. Helmet off, eyes closed, lounging inside the Vector I could be anywhere in the world. Weariness floods my veins, and as my body rests and my mind unwinds, I am filled with longing for the green fields of Kent. I can see them, smell them, feel the tall grasses whisper as I run my hands through ears of seed. I hear bees buzzing in wildflower meadows in summers far past that exist now only in memory. To be away — anywhere — to throw down my helmet and unclip my armour, to lie down on summer-warmed grass and sleep for days and years until I have forgotten the blood and the fear, and the relief when the helicopter takes off again. I want nothing more in the world than this. But Afghanistan cannot be daydreamed away, the Danish mission outside continues, my patrol keeps watch, and my half hour rest is gut-wrenchingly short.

Ngabo climbs down, and my helmet goes on, I put my feelings away inside a box inside a safe, locked and double-locked, hidden away inside a heart of stone, and once again I am a soldier. I climb behind the gun and take up sentry, watching cars passing along Highway One in the distance, counting them as they dip into low ground and pass from sight, and making sure they rise again with Highway One, and continue their journey on the road.

Activity from behind me, the Danish are returning to their armoured vehicles. Doors close, engines roar. Radios chatter to each other, codewords are exchanged, and we are heading back to Bastion to bring them in. The Vector races to the front of the column, I lean into my gun, and wind at my back we patrol for the wire. A sticker on the map marks where we cross Highway One, tracks behind us in the dust show where we have been, and from my vantage point I steer us, talking to the driver over the radio, telling him where I see rocks that could mark an IED, marks on the ground, tire tracks coming together in a choke point, ground that could be too soft. The patrol commander decides the direction, but I decide our side-steps, where we will place our tires and where we will avoid.

We make our way back to the dirt-packed road overlooked by the northern sangars. The column races in, and Bastion looms closer. Now we are in the shadow of sangars, and soon we pass through the front gate and our patrol is done. We stop inside the wire, unload weapons, and make our way to the work yard to refuel the vehicles. We have around six hours before we will go out again, on another mission and another patrol.

42. LASHKAR GAH

The poppies are standing tall in the fields, and flocks of morning birds flood through the airspace in migration as the year wakes up and stretches. The grey mud of winter is all but gone, still lingering on the south sides of ditches but fading fast. With the birds' return, so too comes light — blinding, yellow, dazzling light that soaks everything in sunray and transforms the world from the bitter winter into the promise of the new season, of change, things yet to come; and even the thought of home starts to creep into the minds of our soldiers.

On just such a day the war continues in small packets of brutality, and I find myself again in the IRT tent, awaiting a call. I have come in from a routine night patrol in a WMIK that had consisted of slowly moving down to the bottom of the wadi to watch the silent fields close to Nad Ali, then up to Highway One to stand on sentry until dawn. I find myself, tired and dusty, lugging my kit from Wyvern Lines to the rows of tents where our ready room is housed. I push open the tent flap, and lumber my way in.

I doze, on the 'ready' team, Bella ready and boots on. As mid-morning comes 'IRT this is ops,' breaks on the radio.

We land next to Highway One, the sun high in the sky

and desert opening up away to the south of us, dunes and a small village away to the north. The village where the contact is taking place must be two or three kilometres away, so as we fan out into fire positions I take a knee rather than going fully prone. Bella is resting on my thigh, steadied atop with a hand. From the ISAF vehicles ahead of me comes the casualty, an Afghan boy, being carried by a medic. As they come closer, I see that his grimy face is streaked with tears. There is no need for a stretcher, the child is so small he can be carried with ease by one woman, even with armour on. Her little bundle is snivelling and sobbing, and I think 'How can so much blood come from something so small?' His clothing is stained so dark it looks black; he has taken a bullet to the stomach. The medic has latex gloves to protect her from his blood, but he's leaking blood like a sponge. It is running down her arm and falling in drips to dry on the desert stones below, mixed with his tears. An Afghan man accompanies her — the boy's father. They pass me, and the boy is handed over to the IRT medics. We get called in, but before we can leave the Afghan man must be searched so I take a knee again, facing outwards whilst Chalky rummages around in the Afghan's waistband and armpits, making sure he is unarmed and we can bring him aboard. We fly him to the hospital in Lashkar Gah, I am sitting next to the Afghan man, who looks out of the porthole window the entire trip.

That night I dream I am back on the same flight again, rushing the boy to Lashkar Gah through wind currents of treacle and quicksand. He dies in my dreams, every time, like he died in the cool spring air whilst his father watched out of the window.

We drop his corpse off at Lash, and his father too. The flight back from Lashkar Gah is a lazy one, a quick jump into the air, springing up over Nad Ali then gently, gently, drift down like a feather to whisper into a touchdown on the flight line. I am transfixed by shadows of the boy's death all the way back — the drops of blood on the floor at my feet, the wrappings for IV needles and fresh dressings, scattered casually, carelessly across the airframe's work bay to be cleaned off and sanitised back in Bastion. When they are cleaned off and tidied away, there will be no outward sign he was ever here. The boy's face is seared into my mind, and the war continues.

It started slowly, but before long I was retreating inside myself for hours, even days at a time. Every minute, every second grates on my nerves. The yellow lights of the IRT tent irritate me, the banal chatter of my comrades infuriates me, so I lie on my bunk, arms folded, glaring at the ceiling. The day passes around me as if I were a mere observer. I clean my weapon in silence, eat my food in silence. The days trickle by, we attend O-Groups in teams, gathering around the boss in one of the accommodation tents to hear the day's news. Disinterested, I pretend to write, whilst others are noting down how many 107mm rockets were fired at a FOB in Musa Qala, or in which district of Nad Ali an Afghan National Policeman stole a motorcycle. Dismissed from O-Group, I return to my bunk and stare at the ceiling.

43. CONFESSIONAL

Several days later, the padre is sent to see me. Still on IRT duty, he takes me to the smoking area through the rear flap of the tent. He sits me down on a bench and leans back, surveying me. The rest of the team have gone to lunch, so there's only four men in the IRT tent, right at the far end where they won't be able to hear us. The padre smiles, and his job begins.

'What's your name, son?'

I grudgingly admit that sometimes people call me Charles.

'Charles, your Corporal is worried about you. Is there anything you want to talk about?' He glances at his watch nervously.

'Not really.'

'I understand your friend was killed recently?'

I feel my stomach tighten and a knot rise in my chest. Not killed, I think. Murdered. I look into the sky and think about what it must be like to be a bird. To be able to forget the responsibilities and the weariness of living and just fly, free, into the clear blue sky.

'Yes, but I'm trying not to think about it. Just getting on with the job.' That's what I'm supposed to say. That's what soldiers say, isn't it? I have never felt less like a soldier as I sit with the padre, like an errant schoolboy with the teacher, so kind and understanding instead of being angry, trying to help me instead of punishing me.

'Would you say you're under a lot of stress?'

I feel my emotions, kept at bay for so long, flooding back. This man actually cares, I think, he wants to help. Why not let him? I am in two minds; I don't know how I'm going to answer. Perhaps I will tell him everything, like a confessional. It seems to work for people on TV who confess things to a priest. I might confess to him how I think of all the dead and dying I have seen and my growing fear that they died for nothing. About the ambivalence of my casual disdain for life during the IRT shout, yet my nightmares of watching the day's dead die all over again. I might confess that I've deprogrammed myself from the nonsense they told us in deployment training about woman's rights and reconstruction and fighting the drug trade. I might confess how I gave up wanting to kill to take revenge for Chris dying, because we have killed so many out here already, what does it matter who pulls the trigger on the life-ending round? I might confess that I just want to go home and pull the duvet over my head, to shut out the outside world and sleep until I have forgotten everything that has happened out here. I might even confess the biggest secret of them all, the one that no-one out here is supposed to say or think. That we shouldn't be here at all, taking sides in a civil war, and it's eating me up not being able to tell anyone. I don't know how I'm going to answer him when I open my mouth but just at that moment, he looks at his watch again. He must be missing his lunch.

'Yes,' I hear myself say 'but I'm dealing with it my own way.'

He presses the point though. 'But your Corporal said that you're not eating much or sleeping well.'

I try not to look him in the eye. I stare at the ground between our feet as I decide how to answer. I will give him a test. I will tell him about the nightmares and if he doesn't judge me, if he is kind and caring like the priests in the movies, I will confess everything, unburden myself and pretend to believe in his God so that the priest can forgive me and then I can forgive myself.

'Well,' I say slowly, 'I've been having nightmares.' I look up at him to see how he will take it, how he will coax me to open up, to tell him everything. I want him to, need him to. He thinks about this, his head cocked to one side, looking at me. Then he smiles.

'We all have bad dreams from time to time. After all, this is Afghanistan.' He smiles at me again, to show me his caring and non-judgemental nature, then 'Thanks for talking to me. If there's ever anything else you want to talk about, come and find me.' He stands up and leaves.

I sit a while under the perfect blue canopy, looking up at the sky, trying to become a bird.

44. SOUTH

We assemble as usual around the shipping container of the vehicle yard to wait for 1 Platoon's patrol to return. The cloudless sky seems to herald another baking hot day, and we idle under the piercing blue canopy, sending blue smoke drifting up from our cigarettes and watching birds flying south, into the wind. Half an hour passes by easily, and soon enough we hear the nearby rattle of vehicles bouncing along the dirt road of Bastion, hidden from view by shipping containers and Hesco walls. The platoon kicks up dust as they roll to a stop and jump out, and within a few minutes vehicles are refuelled, water stocked, batteries in the radios changed, and after an ammunition check 2 Platoon have taken over.

One WMIK and the Vector roll out within minutes, I am in the Vector with Fisk top cover in the WMIK. On this day, however, we don't get as far as the main gate before Zero calls us back to lines with a command over the HF radio. We are to pick up a camera crew before we leave. I roll my eyes when I hear they were going to be riding with me in the Vector, despite the reporter being a pretty blonde. Attachments mean trouble, as the patrol commander would be sure to take us somewhere dangerous to impress them.

No northern patrol for us today — today we will be heading down south, I can feel it in my bones and my heart sinks.

◇ ◇ ◇ ◇ ◇

The camera crew's eyes are like saucers as they pull their armour on, perch helmets atop their heads and listen to the patrol commander brief them on the patrol. They are to stay in the vehicles at all times, and if we come into contact, don't get in the way as we do our jobs. Suitably awed by the tough-talking infantry, they load themselves up into our wagons, and away we head. My fears are confirmed as we head out of main gate and swing into the sun, heading east towards the central wadi which will take us south.

Within half an hour, we have pushed south east, over the eastern wadi and up onto the plateau that will slowly drop down onto the plains of Nad Ali. We are taking a new route, pushing further east across the plains to Gereshk before we swing towards Nad Ali. We pass a familiar field system which we drove through about a week ago, at night, farmers' guard dogs bounding from the fields to snarl and bark at us until a well-placed mini-flare drives them away. Beyond the field, the landscape is new to us all and I don't like it one bit. Further and further we drive, east by south east, now south by south east, creeping our way closer and closer to the edge of AO Robin and the population of Nad Ali.

After a while of passing denser and denser compounds though the hills and vales, we come across a Pashtun village, although this far south there is no real desert anymore, just denser or sparser compounds. We are closer to the canal than ever before, fully into the outskirts of Nad Ali. The mud brick compounds are not the larger walled affairs we know from the villages in the wadi, with irrigation channels joining small field systems and farmers standing in their doorways to watch us pass. These are smaller mud-hut style buildings, cramped and close together, with urban detritus of bicycle wheels and corrugated tin spilling into the foot-beaten tracks. The woman and children run like startled deer when we approach, scuttling into their houses and calling to each other. My mind is working overtime, as I see potential firing points everywhere I look, every doorway and corner and alleyway. I check my GPMG is cocked, safety off, and visualise firing without hesitation if I see a target. The whole patrol is getting restless now too. Radio chatter drops off, and instead of the usual relaxed radio messages the drivers exchange terse, curt instructions to move wider for cover, keep distance in case the ground gets softer, close up. From ahead by a line of palm trees that runs along a deep irrigation ditch rises a plume of black smoke. The greenery is denser here, trees and fronds and cultivated and wild. We're at the edge of the Green Zone.

Chalky comes over the radio to the boss, 'See that smoke, boss? Big combat indicator. Maybe we shouldn't hang around here.'

The boss seems unconcerned. 'Burning tyres to alert Taliban to our presence. They did that when I was in Gereshk at FOB Keenan. It's just a crude signal.'

I can barely believe how unconcerned he is. Here we are, two vehicles, miles from any friendly troops, and he wants to kick the hornets' nest, stir up trouble, wait for the Taliban to see us coming and ambush us like they did to Eski's patrol a few years ago. There's a live round I keep behind my plate for emergencies — a 5.56mm bullet, stowed safely in my body armour, in case the worst should happen. If we're over-run, or about to be captured, I will load this round by hand into the breach of a cocked Bella, spin her round, place the muzzle in my mouth, close my eyes against the tears and, heart in my throat, pull the trigger. I rehearse this drill in my head often so that if it comes to it, I won't hesitate — the golden rule out here is: don't get taken alive.

The boss has seen enough. 'Alright boys, spin her for home.'

Relief courses through me, although we are not safe yet by a long shot, but at least we're not crossing the canal, not

going deeper into Taliban territory. As we power away —
the drivers need no second urging — the distance to Bastion
ticks down, the distance we'd have to fight through villages
to get to the open desert and relative safety decreases, and
little by little I feel more relaxed. I am still working hard,
ranging compounds, checking my arc as I face away south,
watching the road we have just taken. A pair of Sea Cobras
thud through the air at low level, making a pass over us and
heading for a contact somewhere — perhaps the new FOBs
that we established in southern Nad Ali, close to Lashkar
Gah, or maybe further to the east, around Gereshk. It's a
comforting sight, knowing that we have firepower like that
minutes away, and now that we are safe again, I feel ashamed
of my nervousness of a few minutes ago. I resolve to be
braver next time we head south, to force myself to believe
that we'd win any contact, instead of drilling myself for the
worst.

45. GERESHK

Another day comes, and another. The routine is tired and familiar. The heat floods and ebbs, we chatter and sleep, day and night pass and our lives float by, whilst we wait.

'IRT this is Ops.'

Our Land Rover races and snakes to the flight line, rotor note building in our ears as we approach. Bella is oiled and ready. The tarmac pan is already buzzing with troops — medics and engineers, my infantry team who fly today, as well as ground crew marshalling the scene. It is a chaos of desert camouflage and weapons, teams and equipment, and everyone shouts in turn over the din. We dash aboard the Chinook; I take my usual spot at the rear by the lowered ramp. We lift soon after, the pilot throwing us down into our canvas frame bench with raw g-force as we speed into the sky and begin our flight to the contact.

The days are slipping away, with more days finished than remaining of Herrick 9. Looking back at the land below the lowered ramp I recognise groups of compounds, gullies and ridges, the landscape familiar and comforting, as the patrol backdrop of the last months give way to unfamiliar desert. We cross Highway One heading north east, towards Gereshk or the FOBs around the town. The poppies have stood tall to the sun and shown their faces; pink and white splashes line the villages we pass, beautiful and stark in the undulating stone and earth desert as the rotors thud and air whips past me. I look to my left and see my team immersed in their own private worlds: Vince drumming his fingers on the stock of his rifle and watching back along the flight line, and Conlay adjusting his gloves with his rifle wedged between his legs. The rear gunner is crouched at his M60, the unfamiliar faces of sappers and Danish officers complete the complement of troops stacked up on benches against the body of the helicopter. The rear gunner stands as the helicopter banks and lifts, and he quickly scribbles on the whiteboard.

ISAF CAS x 1. TIC

My heart lurches when I read the brief message — TIC stands for troops in contact. We will be landing in the middle of a firefight, I run through scenarios in my mind so that I won't hesitate to squeeze the trigger if the time comes. We speed through the air — my mouth is dry, and adrenaline and anticipation floods my veins. We're racing along, the desert slipping by, I see the rear gunner raise his 'one minute' finger, then the pilot starts to hard target. We swoop and wheel in the sky, my heart lurching again, thumping harder as our flares deploy with a bang and we start to take ground fire. White smoke and sparks fizz from the countermeasures, and I catch a glimpse out of my opposite porthole of a cluster of ISAF vehicles before we lift again and circle. The pilot tries to land us, we lose height and the rotors whine then we power out and, head down, race away from the contact. A message is shouted down the line, hand to mouth and mouth to ear. My hand shakes on Bella's pistol grip until I interlace my fingers and take a deep breath.

'Contact too heavy. We can't land. Pick up from FOB.'

We jump up high and the pilot wheels us around in a casual, looping arc that points our nose for home. We circle in the overhead for a while, then put down in a FOB. Stretcher bearers with ashen faces trudge up the ramp, their detached stares show their minds are miles away, back in the contact — the solider on the stretcher has a blanket covering his face. We lift again, shooting into the cold Helmand air, wheeling and banking and juddering our way back to the hospital.

There's nothing to do for this solider, who was declared dead by the FOB doctor. I hear later that he was hit in the head by a bullet during an ambush and died instantly. How many families hear that story of their loved one? That it was instant, he didn't even know what hit him? How many will hear the truth, that their sons and husbands, mortally wounded, held on through force of will for a few minutes longer, until they finally sighed their way out of this life on the floor of a Chinook, lying in front of a shy, softly spoken Rifleman who didn't know where to look, and for whom the faces of the day's dead danced in his dreams every night?

46. DRIVING THROUGH NAD ALI OUTSKIRTS

The other WMIK is broken, after being run day and night without rest. We have one WMIK still serviceable, with the Vector as our command vehicle today. We have a third vehicle though, a Snatch Land Rover, an armoured coffin with poor visibility, and sunroof-style flap for the top cover to stand through, with a rifle in his shoulder. The Snatch has not been approved for use in Helmand, since it is designed for city use on metalled roads, and we are in the middle of a rock-strewn desert. The Snatch also has poor under armour, and since the IED threat is high, we are not allowed to use such a dangerous vehicle. Our company OC has other ideas. We have to patrol AO Robin, and we can't go out on foot patrol because we have such a large area to cover. What can be done? We move the kit and equipment from the broken WMIK to the Snatch and deploy out on the ground. I am lucky, I end up as top cover in the WMIK. I am more exposed to the elements, but I prefer having the GPMG as my weapons system. No-one complains or grumbles about the Snatch except Andy, the driver who ends up behind the wheel.

'She's a right bitch,' he says when we stop side by side in

an overwatch position and I ask him how he's getting on.

'Steering's all rotten, I can't get to my ammo if I need it, and I can't talk to the top cover. Right old bitch she is.'

I shrug and spin around from my position as top cover and watch the wadi. We have stopped about five or six miles south of Bastion, having made our way through the undulating valleys that snake away from Bastion to the central wadi. We are now perched atop a patch of high ground in the middle of the yellow day, watching the sparse poppy farming compounds in the wadi to my east, and vehicles driving by.

Nad Ali, held by the Taliban until December when Operation Sond Chara cleared the town south to north, peters out just on the plain to our south, the outskirts thinning and widening until they reach the rock-strewn dunes upon which we are sitting. There is an old, ruined fortification on this high ground, rightly or wrongly called the Russian fort, which we are sitting just in front of. The lure, this close to Nad Ali, to plant an IED in the hope of catching a war tourist might have been enough for the Taliban to plant a speculative device around the fort, so we stay in the vehicles whilst we occupy this piece of Afghanistan. This morning, this land belonged to the Pashtuns. Whilst we are here, it belongs to a united Afghanistan, under President Kharzai. After we have left, driving down in a bone-rattling rush into the wadi, our wheels slipping and engine growling, it will belong again to the Pashtuns, and their Pashtunwali. I take my helmet off, wrap a shemagh around my head to shield myself from the sun, and resume my watch.

◊ ◊ ◊ ◊ ◊

The radio crackles, EWD have their batteries changed, and still we watch and wait. The sun climbs higher. In the heat the wind picks up, breathing miniature dust devils into life down in the wadi. We don't have a patrol brief, it's up to the commander to decide what to do, where to go — we are left to our own devices as far as the British Army are concerned.

After a spell, Andy spits out of the open door to the Snatch. 'Pass me the arse paper.'

Ngabo, head sticking out on top cover disappears into the Snatch. A minute later, Andy steps easily out of the vehicle, saunters to the front, digs a scrape with his entrenching spade, then turns around and drops his trousers.

'What are you doing Andy?' That's Griff, incredulous.

'What does it look like mate? Hahaa ha!' Andy laughs that throaty chuckle of his and resumes defecating in full view of us all, hanging off the grill on the Snatch to keep from falling back into his scrape.

'We're not supposed to leave the vehicles up here, there could be IEDs.'

Andy's only response is to shrug and spit again.

Vince, commander in my vehicle, has an idea. 'Hey Addy, get the 'terp up. He should see this.'

I steer a foot at him to poke at Aziz, who is sitting on the cramped floor of the WMIK amongst the daysacks and ammo. 'Hey mate, we need you. Get your head up.' Aziz, sleeping, wakes and grumbles his way past my legs to the rear of the vehicle, where he opens the door hatch and slides out, looking around to see what is needed of him. We all laugh.

Aziz, wide eyed, sees Andy, who winks at him. 'Alright sweetheart? Hahaar ha!' Shouting and outraged, Aziz climbs back into the WMIK and sulks into the corner. Andy finishes his business, throws a few shovels of earth over the top and clambers back into the Vixen, tossing a roll of toilet paper back to Ngabo as he does so. 'All ready Griff.'

I ready us to move off again, turning on EWD and re-cocking my GPMG. We are about to descend steeply onto the plains, so when Chalky calls a warning, I drop down and sit rattling around on the floor of the WMIK, braced with both arms outstretched on opposite sides of the vehicle racks. My heart is in my mouth as we drop and slide, puffing up dust and rushing down into the central wadi, just before the choke point at the entrance to Nad Ali. Griff wants to take us the western way, creeping up and around the base of the hills before we reach the western wadi, coming back in over the ranges. We've been patrolling close to Nad Ali more often lately, but west leads out onto the plains where the villages we'll be going through are sparse, traffic is rare, and visibility is good.

◇ ◇ ◇ ◇ ◇

We patrol our way west, engines rattling and puffs of dust coughing up from the dry plains. My vehicle races ahead to take the high ground as we climb up out of the wadi, and the trailing vehicles follow. Amongst the corries and dips as we weave our way through the landscape, we come across a small valley, almost hidden until our noses drop and wheels point us towards the low ground. There are tracks, and a compound, melons growing in ruts carved into the stony ground. Sheep cluster around the small farm. A bright green door with iron inlay shows the entrance and looking down into the compound we see women in vivid blue burkhas.

We were due to stop, so we take up position here, looking outwards and guns swung to defend us against any threat. One gun faces back towards the wadi, one towards the plains ahead, and my gun is ready for any fire coming from the farm below, my range slider set to 200m and GPMG cocked and oiled.

Griff checks the radio and calls Zero to report our location. We settle in for an hour or so of watching over the wadi. The sheep don't bother us, the women have disappeared. My hand does not leave the pistol grip of the gun, and I watch my arc whilst Bruce Lee on top cover in the Vector looks back to the wadi, reporting over the radio the activity he sees.

◊ ◊ ◊ ◊ ◊

A bang comes from the farm, and I swing the gun towards the compound, braced to fire and looking for a muzzle flash or smoke. But there is no crack. Rounds flying overhead make a crack, as the supersonic projectile passes by. After the crack, comes the rapport of the rifle, a diffuse thump. No-one is firing at us. The bang comes again, and the green door swings open.

A man, the farmer, swarms out of the compound, striding with purpose towards us. He has no weapon visible, but I am not going to let him get close enough to see if he's wearing a bomb. I call on the radio that we have an Afghan man approaching from the valley, then I release the GPMG and grab a mini-flare, pulling back the trigger and launching it to pass beside him. The green flash stops him in his tracks, and I hold up a hand to let him know not to come closer.

The interpreter is called for, and Griff and Aziz approach him. Aziz shouts in Pashto, and the farmer lifts up his woollen jumper to show his belly, turning around he shows us his back, then satisfied he is not a suicide bomber Griff and Aziz wave him to approach them.

The farmer shouts and gestures with both hands, furious, pointing an accusing finger at our vehicle— no, at me — then pointing back towards his farm. Chalky chips in over the radio. 'He thinks you're after his melons, Addy!'

The farmer rants for a while, and Aziz shouts back at him. Griff says a few words now and then to Aziz, but mainly the two Afghans argue between themselves. Then the farmer spins, grabs his hat from off his head and marches back toward his farm.

Griff tells us over the radio: the farmer doesn't like that we can see his wives. From up on the high ground we can look in his compound and it compromises the modesty of his women. Griff was having none of it. We need the high ground; he'll just have to keep his wives inside until we're gone.

We leave our position as the winds pick up, blowing in rains ahead of them to turn the melon farmer's channels into lush pools, feed the poppy fields and swell the banks of the river Helmand. We patrol back in file, with two vehicles line astern and one out to the side, for good all-round firepower. We needn't have bothered. The Taliban in our AO are bomb makers and rocket launchers, and the longer we are here the more we realise that they don't plan to shoot, only to try and bomb us on the roads or when we sleep. Before long we are back in camp, where I will be coming off patrols and going on to sangar duty.

47. NIGHTFALL IN THE WADI

The warmth of the day gives way to ember-red dusk and the call of the muezzin, and softly, slowly, blue tinges rise in the east of that inverted bowl we call the sky. Down in the wadi, a breeze from the north chills the shoulders of the scattered poppy farmers, finishing the day's work as night falls and the half-moon rises. We have been out since the hottest part of the day, and now my patrol has crawled under cover of darkness to an observation position in the hills across the wadi, around four kilometres from the steel wire of Camp Bastion that marks the border into this Taliban heartland.

As the night takes hold, we watch and wait. Far distant, the massive shadows of the northern mountains darken and are lost from sight. The nights are slower to cool now, the day's heat lingering into the dark until the edges of cold nudge their way in. I shift Bella slightly in my shoulder, searching in vain for a comfortable position. Silence reigns around us, each man an island of loneliness, lost amidst his thoughts. Miles distant, the other side of the gulf of the night-time wadi, the white, yellow and orange lights of Camp Bastion twinkle softly through haze, whilst we lie on our bellies and stare out into the gloom. To my left, the patrol commander watches too, every so often lifting a radio handset to his head to softly confirm with the ops room that we can still hear them and still haven't moved.

Under the vastness of the night sky alone with the silence of watchfulness, an ambivalence of peace and unease steals across me. Peaceful, beautiful night time in the desert — who could remain unaffected by the vast landscape? From the rocky mountains sweeping down into rolling desert dunes and stony plains as far as the eye can see; with the giant scar of the wadi across the centre of the landscape, punctuated by the lone lights of compounds to our south in Nad Ali. The lights get denser and softer as you raise you sight until the horizon is just an orange glow like a burning city. Amidst the scattered lives in our sparse patch of desert, overwhelmed by the empty space, I feel smaller than ever, a brief spark of life in the tinderbox, to be lost as easily and quickly as I came. Darkness before, darkness after, and the indifference of the empty desert to mark my passing.

The unease of my place in the world mixes with the danger of the unknown. The night hides much, and the same blanket that I am using to hide myself also conceals the deeds of those who we watch for — the Taliban who launch 107mm rockets into camp do so from the wadi, which is a known resupply route into Nad Ali. Perhaps a different band of Taliban, or perhaps the same, are known to run guns, ammunition, and fighters into Nad Ali under cover of night too. The new FOBs in the town are beleaguered from their assaults. So we watch, and wait.

In the past I have patrolled out with Bella loaded but un-oiled- she'll see a good burst from dry without fouling, and a quick squirt from my oil bottle only takes a second. But tonight, she is dripping with oil, my special box with the first ten tracer rounds loaded and ready. We have calculated our rates of fire carefully, I have enough ammunition for four minutes rapid fire from Bella, then twenty minutes of GPMG fire from the gun in the Snatch Land Rover behind us. The stones, cold and hard against my legs and crotch dig in and rattle when I shift. My chest, flat against my armour lies atop a sweat-soaked t-shirt, sucking heat from me. I have a shemagh around my neck to see away the night chills, but as another half hour wears on, I struggle with my task. Weariness, hunger, the cold, and boredom all compete to drag me down and drown me in the sea of indifference, to lapse my concentration. You should sleep, my body whispers softly to me. I can't, I reply, and bite my cheek to stay awake. Yes, we can still hear you. No, we haven't moved. I flex my fingers against the stiffness and the cold, blink my eyes awake and watch. The night wears on.

◊ ◊ ◊ ◊ ◊

'Standby standby,' urgent and hoarse is whispered down the line. Griff has seen something. Down in the wadi, a few hundred metres away, moving shadows. Men? I shift quietly to bring my weapon to bear in the direction. Through night vision we survey them: twelve or so men, moving rapidly towards us, with rifles. My pulse leaps and my mouth is dry. Vince is on one side of me, Ngabo watches from the weapon tower of the WMIK. Perhaps they have seen us? Perhaps there are more of them? They are coming right at us. I quickly look left and right through my night vision scope, although Ngabo should be providing all-round defence from his position in the WMIK. Wait, there's more of them! To our right, only 100m or so, I see a vehicle. I am about to call out to Vince when through the night vision scope I see two flashes from the headlights; yet my other eye, open, sees nothing. Black light! IR headlights, they must be ISAF.

'Vince!' I call, 'Friendlies to our right, given us an IR flash.'

Like lightning Vince leaps up and dashes over to Ngabo's wagon. I lower my weapon from pointing it at the new troops and turn to see the first troops, moving across the wadi through my scope. From this range they are almost on us, and I can see IR glow sticks in their helmets.

'It's the Yanks,' someone calls to Griff.

'Stand down,' Griff calls to us and the fire team echo the call down the line, but stay on their bellies with weapons trained just in case. Vince meanwhile has flashed our own IR headlights at the vehicle to our right, and he and I are to go forward and check them out. Vince walks forwards with both arms in the air, his rifle pointing at the sky. Bella is too heavy to hold upright in one hand, so I hold her far away from my side, pointing at the floor, with my left hand held high. Without the night sight we see only the darkest of shadows.

'ISAF,' Vince calls out. 'Hey buddy,' is the reply.

We make our way to the voice and find a team of Americans in all-round defence around their vehicle. They are obviously Special Forces, the leader has a large bushy beard, baseball cap and all sorts of non-standard kit. He calls down to the team in the wadi on a radio, then we introduce ourselves to him with a handshake.

'Vince, Corporal, 1st Battalion Rifle Regiment.'

'Addy, Rifleman, the same.'

'Kenny,' is the introduction from our new friend. Kenny beams at us, insanely cheerful. 'What are you doing on our RV? We flashed IR at you a few times, we were about to shoot you.'

'I only just saw your flash,' I tell him.

Vince tells him our mission, since they are Special Forces. 'We're supposed to be interdicting Taliban supply routes. This wadi is used a lot to transport arms and men.'

'You don't say,' says Kenny dryly. I suspect that Kenny's men are on task for pretty much the same thing. Kenny is still pretty cheerful about the whole thing. 'Your unit didn't tell you we were operating out here tonight? We told the Brits at briefing today. Still, an IR flash is better than a muzzle flash, huh?'

By this time the team in the wadi have arrived at the RV

and we make our way back to Griff's kill group. We wish Kenny good luck.

'Happy hunting, Brits,' floats back as the Special Forces team slips away into the shadows.

Griff decides to abandon our ambush, and we mount wagons to make our way back to camp. Vince is livid with the boss. 'We could all have been killed tonight by the Yanks, all because our officers are too stupid to arrange a piss up in a brewery.'

'Do you think our lot knew?' I ask him. 'Perhaps the Yanks told someone but not us.'

Vince vents. 'Oh, they knew all right. He thought, "Maybe I should tell Griff that US special forces are operating in our AO. Maybe I should tell the Americans that my men will be out in the wadi tonight. No, I'm too useless and lazy to do my job", and we nearly died because of it.'

Ngabo gets the full force of his ire on the drive back to camp though, as he should have been watching all around, seen the American vehicle approach the hill, and seen the IR flashes long before I did.

We patrol back to camp, with glaring yellow light beaming into the darkness, to sleep through the day. We have another few night patrols and though we will watch all around us through night vision in coming days, we see nothing of Kenny and his team again.

48. THE TUNNEL

I am late to O-Group, the evening's warmth clings on longer into the dusk, and Herrick 9 is starting to wane as the year ages around us. I creep into the admin tent and squeeze in amidst the throng of soldiers, taking a knee between cot beds and the bodies of my comrades. The boss ignores my arrival and continues his briefing. The Rifle Regiment have had a bad day, three men dead in an IED blast that tore their vehicle apart. Three stories that had barely started left with no ending, and tomorrow — today — three sets of visiting officers will sit in their car, hearts in their boots, for a second longer than necessary before they make that longest walk to a front door. The three men were providing protection to a convoy along Highway One to Gereshk, just past our front doorstep, when a culvert packed with explosives was detonated. It was the largest IED to date in Helmand, and an ill omen of days to come.

Tomorrow's task is IED hunting in the culverts in our AO, to clear them by hand. Jacobs, Fisk and I join Griff, Ngabo, and Vince. Griff calls us to stay behind as he gives us a pre-patrol briefing. We will clear the culverts from west to east. The IED searcher will clear a path up to the tunnel with the metal detector, then swap the Vallon for a pistol, get on his belt buckle, and crawl inside to check for bombs. Fisk will take close protection duty for the Vallon man. We are dismissed with eight hours until the patrol goes out. I strip off in my cubbyhole, shake foot powder into my boots, dust down Bella, and crawl into my sleeping bag.

◊ ◊ ◊ ◊ ◊

I sleep until the early hours, woken by Conlay. Whilst the sentries in their sangar struggle through their death stag, and long before the camp awakes, we prepare. Fisk is repacking his link into a respirator case for easier access, Vince is swapping over kit between daysacks, and Jacobs is cutting elastic strips off his helmet. We all busy ourselves with something: my job this morning is to scavenge some food from the communal boxes in the tent entranceway. I rummage through MREs, chicken powder noodles and flavoured rice bags, and gather enough food for the patrol. We amble across to the vehicle handover point in small packets. I am the last to arrive, as I dash into the wash block for a quick shave just before we head out. The wagon handover takes only a few minutes, and when water is replenished, fuel levels checked, ammo accounted for, and GPMGs signed over — the Vixen is mine again. I double-check everything, the batteries, the spare batteries, the water, I wedge my daysack in beside the radio and wedge myself in the back behind armoured doors. Bella sits across my knees and the patrol rumbles off.

◊ ◊ ◊ ◊ ◊

The sangars stand tall flanking the gateway to Bastion 2, towering above us like the poppies standing tall in the fields. Thousands of hours of dreams and memories have aged them, our towers of solitude where we hold the line between our fortress and the deserts. In one hundred years, will they be here still, guarding nothing, holding empty dreams and memories, whilst the world ages around them? Our vehicle patrol drives between the steel gates that open between them. As we pass through, the lonely silhouettes of the sentries are just visible — unknown, faceless — they might as well be a hundred years away from us as we head out to the culverts. They are locked in their own private war, walking their own road as we walk ours. The dust rises from the road under the WMIK's wheels, and I lean into my gun from the rear vehicle, rocked and buffeted from side to side as we bounce over the desert's baked earth. As we speed onto the rough road leading us to Highway One, the drivers put the engines to the test and the wind chills me. It whips around my face and spits up sand and dust to wreath my head like a halo. Our objective is to the north, but first we swing to the west, patrolling along and crossing Highway One, before dropping down into the cover of low ground around the small wadis on the north side.

Our patrol sees in the dawn, and as the light opens another day we retreat onto the northern plains. The desert expanse closes in and hems us with dunes and hummocks, small hills and valleys, and we double back on ourselves, stop and go into all-round defence and prepare for the next phase of the operation. I swing my gun outwards and rest my chin on the back of my hand on the stock of the gun as Chalky wheels the Vixen to align with the WMIK. There isn't much to see in my arc, just the grey-green bushes that hang on to crevices and the ochre of Helmand in ever-lightening tones from here to the horizon, and from there many times beyond sight. Griff finishes his brief with the drivers, then they come up to the guns and take watch whilst Jacobs, Fisk and I are called in for a briefing. Griff hefts a pistol in his left hand absent-mindedly, with a map in his right. The orders don't take long; we will drive up as close as we dare, then one of us will jump out and sweep with the Vallon, marking a clear path to the first culvert, with a machine gunner following four steps behind him for close protection. Then the tunnel man will clamber into the concrete drain under the highway, swapping the metal detector for a cocked pistol, and crawl through alone to meet the patrol on the far side, checking for IEDs.

Jacobs or I, as top covers, are the choices to sweep the culverts. I remember back to when Operation Lava went out at night in the pouring rain, and I cleared a path with my feet. Since then we have stopped more times than I can count and cleared vulnerable points. At choke points, where the ground funnels you to a particular path, we sweep and clear with the metal detector before the vehicles move through. Jacobs though barely waves the detector head left and right before he calls the ground clear. I don't trust him to do a good job, and before I can think about what I'm saying, I have volunteered to clear the culverts. Griff frowns, furrowing his craggy face, not expecting a volunteer for IED clearance duties, but he accepts anyway, and the Vallon and pistol are mine.

Fisk follows me warily, stepping in my footprints as we make our way to the tunnel. I take a meandering route, avoiding the obvious approach to the entrance. The crisp, clear day is shaking off the chill of night quickly, and the bright sky looks inviting. I am at the entrance to the culverts. No going back. I pass the Vallon to Fisk, drop into a crouch and pistol in hand, clamber my way inside the tunnel and into the dark gulf beyond.

The sounds of the desert plains die quickly, muffled then extinguished as I crawl on my stomach through the darkness. Now deeper in the tunnel, there is only the sound of my breath rasping as I struggle onwards. With elbows and knees, I drag myself through the concrete pipe. The back of my helmet catches my armour when I try to raise my head and look forward, and I have to lift my body up with my hands, bending backwards at the waist to see fully ahead. I scrape and push my way onwards, through dried mud caking the floor of the tunnel that cracks and breaks as I pass through. No-one has been in here since before the rains, at least. It has taken me minutes, and I am not yet halfway.

I pause for a few seconds, resting my chin on a balled fist to take the weight of my helmet from my neck, and as I do so there is a growl and a rumble. Then an ear-splitting roar shakes the air, rattling my teeth in my jaw as the world is engulfed in noise and vibration. At first I think we are under rocket attack, but as the roar fades only to be replaced by another roar, I realise it must be a convoy passing Highway One above me. Americans or Canadians perhaps, travelling at company strength. I close my eyes and force the tips of fingers into my ears, waiting for the convoy to pass.

When the final rumbles have died away, I breathe again and crawl onwards toward the spot of light that lifts darkness into gloom, and gloom into visibility. I emerge, and Fisk helps me to my feet, brightness pricking my eyes as he hands me back my machinegun.

We clear two more tunnels, each time without incident. Griff beams and calls me '2 Platoon's tunnel rat,' and proud of the compliment, I volunteer for any other tunnel clearance we have to do on the rest of our operations.

◊ ◊ ◊ ◊ ◊

We stay out patrolling the central wadi for a few hours, then make our way back to camp, crossing sewage river and looping around to the south. We cross the ranges on our way, kicking up the thick dust that has settled around the Hesco. The shemagh wrapped around my face keeps the worst of it out but I am covered by the time we cross into camp. I smack the dust from my combat jacket when we are back at lines, spitting through a dry mouth and tasting grit.

We clean weapons, clean ourselves, look after our feet. We shave, change clothes, and put our berets on. If we're quick, we can eat before the evening's memorial ceremony.

The time has come. We march to the memorial cross made from 105mm shell casings that stands outside the ops room. The padre is there before us, and squads from other regiments and corps are arriving too. Two coffins stand before him on wooden frames, each covered with a Union flag. We fall in, on three sides, and stand easy. We wait, and I study the faces on parade around me: Marines, Riflemen, Gurkhas, engineers, medics, and artillery. There are some navy and RAF personnel. Some soldiers have no insignia visible, but thick beards and black jackets, and woollen caps instead of berets. Some of them look angry, some eyes are red. Some look bored and others chew gum. The RSM approaches.

'Stand ready,' comes the low order from the senior Rifleman, and we stand tall, braced and ready.

The RSM stamps to a stop. 'Parade!' he bellows. 'ATTEN – SHUN!' Boots stamp into the dust and we assume the position of attention. Officers arrive, salutes are exchanged, and then, 'Parade! — Stand at — EASE!'

This is the padre's time, and he raises his voice to the air and talks from the diaphragm for all of us to hear, about duty and sacrifice, loyalty and faith, and he promises eternal life in front of the coffins of the corpses. Silence fills the spaces around his words, as we gaze across the parade square. Then the coffins are collected and loaded into the back of ambulances, so we have to assume the position of attention again. When it is all over, we turn to the right, salute, and march off.

We have paraded like this between patrols, around meals, around sentry duty and IRT duty since the start of our deployment. Every time a soldier dies the phones are switched off, and the email at the welfare computer is switched off, whilst the visiting officers break the news to the bereaved family. It is called Op Minimise , and the camp tannoy announces with a crackle every time it is set or repealed. Whilst the communication blackout is in effect, we parade as we have done tonight, to see another coffin dispatched to the flight line and from there to Brize Norton and eventually home.

◊ ◊ ◊ ◊ ◊

We are allowed a few minutes per week welfare call on the satellite phone, if our duties allow and the phones haven't been switched off. But it is nearly a full kilometre from company lines to the communications shack where the shared phones are kept. After a long patrol and looking after my weapon and my feet, cleaning myself and shaving, spending enough time in the wash block to take care of all my daily needs, eating noodles from the welfare box and drinking a cup of tea, the kilometre walk to join a queue for the phones is less appealing than a clean, cold cot bed with a sleeping bag on top. So it is tonight. The phones are back on, but I am too weary to use them, and climb into my time machine, to fast-forward to another day.

49. CLEANING WEAPONS ON
GRANITE 52

The last few hours of night are almost spent, and my weary eyes slide closed for blissful seconds as I take a break from daily cleaning. Daily cleaning is an essential ritual to keep our weapons serviceable, scrubbing off rust with wire brushes, flicking away dust with horsehair brushes, and scraping and polishing and wiping over and over until they are clean enough to attract dust again tomorrow.

We had been patrolling the central wadi close to the airfield, clearing the area under the flight path where the risk of a Stinger missile is greatest to the departing flights.

In the hours before wheels up we cleared the wadi and sat in overwatch as the stars winked into life and the sun settled, and slept sound. When night rolls in we pull fleeces and jackets close, wrap our necks and heads as best we can to protect against the biting cold that still whips around us when the wind blows from the north. Our body armour, tight across the shoulders and biting the waist settle our clothes into the creases where sweat pools in the day and the damp under-clothes wick the heat from your body at night. Our vehicles are battered and beaten, relics before their time, museum-ready snapshot testaments to the Army's supply chain shortages.

We live by halves, here in Helmand. We have one pistol for two men, one morphine syringe each instead of two, and not quite enough bayonets for this patrol to have any. Some soldiers stopped in Kandahar on the way back from R&R and bought fighting knives from the boardwalk, which are strapped to body armour or belts or the side of a daysack. Big Jimmy went out on patrol in a baseball cap last night because his helmet strap was broken, and no-one had the right size bolts to fix it.

Tonight's patrol was short, which means admin time in the welfare tent. Usually we can sleep in shifts until it is time to handover our patrol to the next platoon, or go out again for a flightpath clearance. Tonight though, Griff wants us to clean and service the weapons. So whilst the night wanes and ages before our eyes we sit on wooden benches, scrubbing gas parts, pulling wadded cotton through the barrels, and I close my eyes for seconds at a time and daydream. My body, on autopilot, continues to polish the same gun part I've been cleaning for the last hour.

Am I imagining it, or have the first vestiges of dawn sidled into camp to dilute the darkness that swims around the orange walkway lights? We assemble the guns, oil them and perform function checks, then heave the guns and our kit and our weary selves across the matted walkways that lead out of our lines to where the vehicles are parked. As I am top cover, it's my job to mount the GPMG back on our WMIK. I clamber onto a wheel, haul myself over ballistic armour plates strapped to the bones of the WMIK, and swing my legs into the turret to stand at my post. Fisk hands me up the gun, and I manoeuvre it into place, wiggling steel pins through delicate parts to mould it to the turret, becoming part of the vehicle again. The new day is almost on us, and with only a few hours until patrol hand-over and a blissful twelve hours of stand-down and admin time, we shake ourselves awake.

50. PB TANDA

I slip out of the shelter of the musty IRT tent and sit out back in the semi-shade of the tent's awning. The morning wears on, aircraft howling to a landing or into a climb from the airstrip half a mile east. At this time of day, a few hours before lunch, the town of canvas tents is empty save for the aircrew, the counter IED teams, and the infantrymen on call. I've been sleeping in my boots, on immediate notice to move. At the end of my bunk stands propped my body armour, half open for speedy donning, with my haversack of 800 rounds of 5.56mm link clipped to the waist. My helmet is propped against the bed strut at an angle — easy to grab — and Bella. Bella is clean and oiled for firing, a box of 100 rounds ready in place, with the belt hanging down limp. Because I'm closest to the rear flap of the tent, I've draped a shemagh over her body, to stop dust getting in her guts. And so we wait, kit ready and boots on.

Chalky's Cornish voice floats through the open tent flap, intruding into my thoughts. I don't hear what he said, but laughter from inside the tent follows. Morale is important, but right now I feel cut off from my comrades. I don't want to talk, to eat, to even think or feel anymore. Tired, dirty and numb, I sit on a rickety wooden bench on the gravel, half-shielded from the sun by the perforated awning, cleaning my nails with a pocket knife to distract myself, waiting for lunch or a shout, whichever comes first. It's hard to do, waiting for something which could happen at the next moment, and the more I think about a shout, the more impatient I become. I sit for a moment or two staring at the Hesco wall ten feet in front of me. The sun is creeping high in the cloudless sky, and I'm starting to sweat. I rise and stretch my legs, then walk back into the tent. Halfway along one wall the television is playing another film, the latest Hollywood action film in poor quality, grainy Afghan-copy style. We have seen all the films anyone owns at least twice, but it passes the time. Whilst I was out, Chalky made everyone a cup of tea and mine sits, steaming, by my bed.

here are probably contacts all over Helmand right now, 1 Platoon out on patrol in the AO would most likely be laagered up somewhere with all-round visibility, helmets off, enjoying the freedom of the desert. I feel stuck in this tent, boots on, not even able to have a shower, waiting in vain for the crackle and shout. The sun climbs higher and the cooling fan unit breaks down with a cough. Sweat pools and trickles in the runnels and crevices of the body, we're slowly starting to swelter.

By now, despite the fighting weather heating us through layers of canvas, it feels like a quiet day. As it starts to wear into evening, we will start standing men down, one at a time, for showers or a trip back to Wyvern lines for personal admin. I busy myself with another letter to Charlotte, but even the thought of my own girlfriend doesn't raise my mood right now. All I can see ahead of me is supper, then bed, then another day of waiting for a shout. The despondency is a hard beast to shake, it weighs me down, dragging jokes and smiles and everything good into a place where I exist, and that is all. The television burbles like a drain in the background, and I sink deeper into my own thoughts.

Serjeant Barney sticks his head around the canvas flap that serves as a door, and seeing that he has the right tent, enters and sits down on the spare bunk nearest to the door. He's come to get our report of the day's activity, and take it to the OC. 'Quiet one, is it?' Half the tent groans. The word is taboo.

Chalky remonstrates with Serjeant Barney, 'You've done it now, we'll have two shouts before morning, just you wait. If I get killed on the next one, I'm blaming you.'

Serjeant Barney just shrugs, unfazed by the reaction. 'So nothing today then?' he asks Bazza, the IRT commander.

'Not a peep.'

Chalky hasn't finished though, when he starts setting the world to rights he knows how to go on. 'Ops room, bah! There's probably been twenty shouts, they just forgot to tell us. Like yesterday, we saw the pilots dashing across the tarmac, heard sirens — nothing on the radio. I stand the boys to, just in case, and there's the bird on the tarmac, turning and burning, waiting for us. Bloody joke those lot.'

Serjeant Barney says, 'Well I was in the ops room before lunch, and it was pretty quiet right across province. A few contacts in Musa Qala, one in Nad Ali that already broke, but that's about it. If they forget to tell you again, let me or the boss know. We'll sort it out.'

We relax back into our bunks as Serjeant Barney leaves, to return to his cup of coffee over last week's newspaper back at lines.

◊ ◊ ◊ ◊ ◊

I've nearly finished my letter to Charlotte when the radio splutters a burst of static, followed by the opening lines 'IRT this is ops'. We are being stood to. Measured urgency grips the tent, lives may depend on seconds, much can pivot on such tiny things. Someone is dying, on the cusp between life and death, and we do everything we can to bring them back. I heave my body armour onto my bunk and, sitting down, wedge myself between the plates, buckle the shoulder and tighten the straps. I whip the shemagh off Bella, grab my helmet and dash for the door. People collide and kit trails. I jump into the back of the Land Rover, sliding onto my belly then turn back to have weapons and radio sets passed up to me. Bazza is on the radio to the ops room, gleaning valuable fragments of information about the shout. Bodies clamber helter-skelter into the Land Rover, I feed Bella the starting rounds of her belt of ammo and whilst we're doing this Bazza drops the handbrake and we jolt forwards, surging out and along the dusty road. There are three soldiers in the back of the Land Rover, aligned sideways on benches — myself, Big Jimmy, and a Royal Marine signaller. Chalky in the passenger seat is our team commander, and Bazza will drive the vehicle back and wait to pick us up afterwards. My heart pounds, my dry throat soaks up saliva like a sponge, excitement races through my veins, animating my fingers to tighten their grip on the Land Rover frame.

Bazza shouts back at us after taking a high-speed corner, 'UK!'

Big Jimmy and I look at each other, craning to hear.

'Category A!'

That's unusual. Immediate evacuation, non-surgical.

'That's all we know!'

'Heatstroke,' I shout to Big Jimmy, and he nods and shouts back,

'Silly bugger needs a few pints in him.'

In this heat and carrying the loads we have soldiers will drop like flies without four to six litres of water a day. When we first got here all those months ago, I was drinking six litres a day, in 38-degree heat. I lose my balance as we round another corner at high speed, then accelerate out of the apex, and Big Jimmy laughs as I'm jerked backwards, grabbing at the frame of the vehicle to keep me in my seat. We approach the Chinook flight line at speed, racing out onto the tarmac towards our helicopter, stopping short with another jerk. Four of us jump out, and jog towards the rear ramp, encumbered with our kit. We've arrived fast and are there before the crew have started the rotors up. We clamber aboard and take our places against the hull at the rear of the aircraft. Looking back, I see Bazza in the Land Rover driving off the pad as other vehicles arrive, bringing medics and the Danish Counter-IED team. They too climb aboard, and I put my earplugs in, in anticipation. The rear gunner stands at the ramp with his headset on, talking to the pilots through a microphone, then turns to the side and starts checking dials and pressing buttons on his control panel. With a groan, then a whine, the engines fire and the rotors creak their way faster and faster into a blur. The noise builds, the vibration creeps through everything. I give Chalky, sitting opposite me, the thumbs up and he grins back as we lift into the air. Orientation is lost in a moment as we dip and roll, then yaw left and right as the pilot tests the controls. Then, nose tipped forwards toward the ground and tail high in the air, we lift and turn and accelerate away from camp, buzzing over the central wadi and turning to the south and racing away. The airflow cools us, we must really be making an effort to get there as the desert whips by as we speed onwards, southward, at low level. The rear gunner squats on his haunches and frees his M60, checking the traverse, watching the ground below. A call comes, mouth to ear, down the line. We are going to Patrol Base Tanda.

◊ ◊ ◊ ◊ ◊

The landscape whips by in a rush of colour below us, as we fly faster and lower than on any shouts before. The RAF pilots have given way to Navy, and this one knows how to fly. Within a minute we have passed over the northern edge of Nad Ali and the southern boundary of AO Robin, the canal has bled into the river Helmand and we are following the snaking, shallow water southwards at high speed.

The beauty of this country is striking from this low, the view from the lowered rear ramp shows the close-up compounds of the Green Zone streaking by against a backdrop of the rugged grey mountains away to the north, and every dash of colour against the drab grey and brown of the baked earth is like viewing a human kaleidoscope.

Minutes race by, and at a bend in the river we diverge from following the Helmand and branch off to the east, rising and gaining a little altitude. I think we must be flaring to land, but a treeline shoots past instead and I realise we must have lifted up to clear over it. Chalky opposite me has a wild grin on his face, his eyes wide behind goggles as we lurch in the air. We wheel to the right, and a mud compound with Hesco and barbed wire looms into view out the opposite portholes, then we flare and dust kicks up as we touchdown. We have barely bounced down, and a stretcher is hurried on, within seconds the rear gunner is shouting at the stretcher bearers to get off the helicopter. Outgoing machine gun fire crackles from the PB, we've landed in the middle of a contact. Fear and excitement mix in my veins. I hope that we get away without taking a hit, even small arms fire is a threat — to the helicopter and also the troops in the back who could catch a bullet through the thin metal skin. The rear gunner is kneeling at his M60, both hands on the handles and ready to fire, and without warning the helicopter rises quickly, and shoots up to gain altitude so fast that I feel like I'm going to be pulled from my seat. The whir and thudding of rotor blades all but drowns out the sounds of fighting. As we peel off and rush away northwards, I see the PB for one last time in my life, muzzle flashes pricking out but no enemy in sight.

We skim the ground on the way back, taking a different route, and this time my view from the Chinook is back away south — dense urban sprawl of mud brick homes and greenery, tiny field systems settled into the low ground, with the plains stretching to the horizon and beyond. Far away south is Garmsir, FOB Dwyer and FOB Delhi, and the patrol base which my friend Chris left one bright morning on New Year's Day, and never came back. The casualty lies at my feet, slightly to the fore of the aircraft, unconscious with twin saline drips already pricked into him, one in each arm.

That evening, the O-Group tells us news of the casualty we picked up. He had got dead drunk on smuggled vodka, poisoned himself and slipped into an alcohol coma. Military prison for him for sure, and stern warnings to us all that any alcohol use would not be tolerated. I shrug this threat off; I already drank Maggie's whisky, we held Chris's wake, I have nothing left and Charlotte has sent me only Jaffa cakes and teabags in my latest care parcel. The evening flies are buzzing and the night-time flights from the airfield have already started to roar by the time we finish the O-Group, and just like that another Afghan day is done.

51. POPPIES

In the Helmand summers, the beauty of the Hindu Kush mountain range and the stark, bleak Dasht-e-Margo is challenged by a sight you can only appreciate from a hilltop or mountainside. The days of summer are long, gold and turquoise visions without a cloud to mar the sky. Hot, clear days, with hardly a drop of wind to stir the landscape, and on such a day our patrol makes its way across the high ground of the eastern wadi, and finding the tallest vantage point we can, drive up to the southern edge of the vast rolling dunes to look out south across Nad Ali.

My vehicle is the first of our pair, driving in column, and pointing my GPMG dead ahead from the gun turret of our WMIK, I lounge back against the turret's padding. The high ground of the wadi's plateau ends just ahead of us, and runs down in steep slopes to the plains below, where the towns and villages that had started creeping north from Nad Ali have stalled their progress, coming up against the rise of the hills and the arterial road formed by the vast, wide wadi itself. Haze hangs on the horizon, a purple-grey fuzz, but in the semi-circular half-panorama, we see miles upon miles of ochre compounds dashing the landscape in patches. The blue line of the canal running east–west marks the boundary into Nad Ali proper, and greenery follows the Helmand river to Lashkar Gah and out of sight. Almost everywhere between the compounds half a mile away and the horizon are lush green fields in perfect squares, with white and pink poppy flowers more numerous than the stars.

I had thought of poppies as the soft-stemmed blood-red streaks of crimson, swaying with the breeze in a wheat-field, as Flanders Field poppies of the poem. Not these eastern white and pink opium poppies that grow to waist height and above, vivid and beautiful, foreign yet familiar.

Andy stops the vehicle and whistles over the radio. 'Check it out boys. We're come to a romantic lookout spot. Eh?'

The Vixen rolls up beside us, Jacobs facing rearwards, and he turns around to see the view.

'Lot of money down there I reckon,' says Bruce Lee after a while.

Andy pipes up on the radio, 'If he asks you to take any packages on the flight back home, just say no.'

Bruce Lee is right, the heroin from the poppies that we can see must be worth —

'Must be worth millions,' I say.

'Yeah but you gotta lotta work to do. Refine it. Concentrate it.' Bruce Lee waves his hand around vaguely as he realizes he doesn't know what the heroin refining process involves. 'These poor bastards growing it probably get pennies. It's those rich ones with rolls of dollars the size of your fist who are making the money.'

The sight takes me away from the patrol, away from the army for a moment, as I remember climbing up the Kentish Downs as a child, my sister and I picking blackberries in the hedges on the way up. We would pick handfuls to eat and fill bags to take home. After we had taken enough, we sat on the top of the rolling chalk downs and looked out at the expanse of south Kent laid out before us; fields green and yellow, rapeseed and crops, and the sea shimmering on the horizon.

The déjà vu, almost but not quite the same, familiar but different. I wonder if I can smuggle some poppy seeds back home and grow opium poppies. I have no intention of making opium, but this view, after months of cold winter, the feeling of happiness and contentment that looking out over this beautiful scene has given me, I want to hold onto it; to somehow wrap it up and keep it in a box, to open in years to come when I feel sad or lonely. I wonder if maybe growing a few of these poppies might help me keep that feeling alive in me.

After a minute more Griff tries to call in our position to Granite Zero. 'Granite Zero this is Granite 64.' No reply. 'Granite Zero.' But we are too far south, too far from base, and we have lost comms with the ops room. 'Andy, head back, lost comms, we need to get closer.' And with that we move off north again, to drive down into the wadi and make our way back to camp over the next hour, leaving the sight of the poppies behind us.

Usually I am happy to be heading north and home to camp, but this time a sadness rises up in my chest and catches in my throat. For the first time in weeks I have thought about home , my family as they were ten years ago, my parents, my baby brother, of long summer holidays with bare feet on the lawn, bitter shandies with my father and Starbucks coffees with my mother. If I die out here, how will they explain it to each other? I wonder who will break the news to them, if my mother will see the visiting officers coming up the front path and know what has happened before the doorbell rings. I am almost mourning my own death and I haven't even died yet.

◊ ◊ ◊ ◊ ◊

We snake our way back to camp through the scattered villages, machineguns outwards and eyes on firing points. Empty doorways and flat rooftops are scanned and mistrusted, children held off with palms outwards and weapons ready. Cars cough up dust from behind them as they too negotiate the wadi, and we pop mini-flares to warn them away, and little by little we count down the miles until Bastion rises into view. We slow down — the IED threat is highest at choke points and routes we use often, and the closer we get to camp the warier the drivers get. Line astern, our vehicles chug past the ranges, and under the eyes of the sangars on the south side of camp we swing off the dust and join the main road. More pops, and mini flares fly as we hold back Afghan traffic on our way into camp. I relax slightly as we pass the main gates, and there's a minute to get our helmets off and take a drink of water as Griff checks in with the Ops room to make a patrol report.

Now the tactical part of the patrol is over. We park up in the work yard and GPMGs are unmounted and handed down from the turrets, boxes of link are counted, radio batteries checked, water replenished and daysacks and backpacks moved away. There are a few hours until the next patrol goes out, so we gather in the admin tent, sprawl on benches and camp chairs and strip down the GPMGs, handing parts out so that everyone has a share. Orange dust, tar-like from mixing with gun oil cloys to the innards of the guns, every part has to be wiped down, dusted down, wiped and dusted and dusted and wiped until the signs of desert are removed. Ten minutes are lost this way, then another ten. Then we re-oil the parts, assemble the machineguns, and make our way to 1 Platoon's tent to hand the GPMGs over to the next patrol commander.

52. PATROL NORTH OF HIGHWAY ONE

The wheels turn and the season is dying; we move on, a foreign column in a foreign country, watched by unseen eyes from the desert hills and mountains as we rumble past the cool clay mud-brick houses of the poppy farmers. Their wives and children stand to watch us pass, like vivid cloth-patches of orange, purple and blue against the soft green and pink of ripening poppy fields. The sickly smell of the opium flower dances in the breeze. Stood up in the turret, with just my head and helmet and weary eyes and weapon showing, I am tired but the poppy's delicate pollen brings back memories of my youth, of corn heads waving in the breeze, and long walks through now unfamiliar Kentish woods in the summers as a child. I sigh and wipe the dust and grime from my eyes and look back at the nearest splashes of wives and children, pivoting to watch us like statues on a turntable. I wave at them as we roll onwards, but no-one waves back. There is no sign of the men.

We cross the wadi, moving parallel to Highway One, creeping our way up and over and around the tiny dunes scattered at the bankside. We are in no hurry. The desert is wide; the desert is old. Time is one thing that is in ample supply out here. Our patrol moves into some dead ground around the dunes, to sneak our way closer to the highway, before taking up an overwatch position. The village behind us is lost to sight. It may have been swallowed up by the desert for all we would know. These are our final days in the country, and everything we do seems to be crossing another marker, another milestone, another day in the countdown until we leave this place behind. When we are gone, for all they know here, the desert may as well have swallowed us up too.

◊ ◊ ◊ ◊ ◊

We make our way east, towards Gereshk, passing the Russian minefields. As we climb a ridge, the WMIK ahead stops; Jacobs has seen something. I turn from my gun turret to see — a vivid gash striping across the desert floor, a road of vehicle tracks. Armour and wheels have churned up the ground, throwing up dust and gouging out a path. Who is this unit that has crossed our AO? It must be ISAF, the tank tracks scattered amidst the wheel ruts show them to be, like us, a foreign column in a foreign land. We follow the tracks south, crossing Highway One to the east of Catford.

As we drive we come to a farm, a small, lonely compound, with an Afghan man sitting despondent in front of his orange painted door. Boys play around him as he sits, staring out at his field. Where yesterday were dull green stems topped with streaks of pink and white opium poppy, today his field is stripped bare, churned up by tractor wheels, and matted with charred, dead poppy stems. A thin black smoke still smoulders from the pile of his burned crop. He turns his eyes to us as we approach, and holds my gaze, as his sits amongst the remains of his year's work.

One of the boys picks up a stone and cocks his hand back. Jacobs spins his gun and reaches for the cocking lever. I grab for the radio.

'Gun forward, mate. I've got these covered.'

Jacobs drops his hand and looks at me accusingly from his turret. I glance, then turn away, but I can feel his eyes on me whilst I watch over the Afghan man and his boys. The boy lets the stone drop to the floor from his hand and turns back to play with his brothers.

The same black smoke rises from a dozen other fields we pass, as we follow the tracks south.

Finally, we find them at the base of a dune, a cluster of tractors, tanks, Jackals, WMIKs, and Vectors, with a sentry vehicle atop the dune watching away south towards Nad Ali. They have laagered up in all-round defence and see us coming, their commanders move out of the ring of armour to meet us.

They are PEF — the Poppy Eradication Force — made up of ISAF, British and Afghan troops. They are working through our AO to Nad Ali, burning opium crop on the way.

We stop here for a time, helmets off, safe beneath the watch of their sentries before they fire their engines into life and churn up the dust towards Nad Ali. Turning west again, we patrol back to Bastion, and towards home.

53. SIGINT REPORT

Jamshed and I are in the back of the Vector, sitting next to the small radio. Our vehicle patrol moved out under cover of darkness, hurrying east before the crisp, cool night gave way to the first rays of the day's baking heat, and Nad Ali began again to stir. We have three vehicles laagered up in all-round defence, on the high ground above Nad Ali. Our newly-repaired WMIK is back in action, and the patrol consists of a pair of WMIKs keeping watch fore and aft, with the Vector in the middle. We are on the high plain in the south east of our AO, far enough away that the hill crest keeps us out of view of the town, but close enough to intercept radio communications from the Taliban, using UHF radios. The high plain is a dust and stone desert, criss-crossed with hummocks and hills, hidden corries and dips, and we are well hidden from any except those well-off the tracks. There is no-one around to see us, and no-one to see.

Vince came up with the plan himself, to use the antenna fitted to the Vector, and wire it up to a tiny UHF radio instead of the battered army communication HF radio. Then we sneak our way close to Nad Ali, and with the increased range try to listen in to anything useful of the Taliban's communications. After a few minutes, we found a frequency in use. Jamshed is our interpreter today, he translates the foreign, distorted voices we hear chattering away, and I am scrawling his words in my notepad as fast as my cramped hand can write.

Long silences come and go, as each voice cuts in, sends their message, and then is lost.

Half an hour passes of sparse chatter, and we discover nothing useful, except Talib Amidullah is addressed in formal Farsi, instead of Pashto, and is probably the leader of the group using our frequency.

The top covers are stood down in turns to get a brew and let the commanders take watch behind the guns, and drivers sit behind the wheel and crack open their stolen American rations to snack on whilst we wait.

Messages come and go, until from the radio breaks a sound unlike any I have ever heard. It is closest to the muezzin call, a sing-song warble like a lark, ever changing note and tone.

Jamshed smiles. 'He is singing a Naat. It is a traditional song.'

The Taliban singer's voice rises and falls, ebbs and flows, a beautiful voice singing a song of his homeland. The hairs on my neck rise to hear it, so strange and foreign, sung in mysterious unknown words yet haunting and beautiful. The young singer's high tenor is like a child's voice, and it saddens me to think that he would kill me given the chance, and I him. The Taliban, like us, listen on in silent appreciation, for no-one cuts in with radio chatter to disturb the melody. A minute later, the song ends and the spell breaks. The radio crackles again with messages, and Jamshed translates,

'They are all asking where he went, and complimenting his voice. They are right, these Taliban. He did have a lovely voice.'

Silence for minutes longer. Then slowly, gradually, like a rising tide the chatter picks up apace. Quari has brought the things to the place they were at yesterday. Talib Amidullah will not be there, but he wishes blessings on them. They are waiting. They have the things they need. Now they are moving to the new place they talked about yesterday. Where is Sher Agha? He is here, on his way. One of them can see the unfaithful moving towards them now. They are ready.

Griff calls Zero to tell them we can hear an ambush being prepared for ISAF troops. Zero wants to know more. 'Whereabouts?' Griff can't say, somewhere in or around Nad Ali, or possibly Gereshk.

'Can you give any more information?' I press Jamshed to give us something, anything, that will help us know where they are and warn the unit. Jamshed shrugs and continues translating,

'God bless you, come on.'

'They are coming.'

And then, 'Go to the other channel. Do not use this channel.'

Then silence.

We scan up and down through frequencies, but only find a pair of lorry drivers in convoy talking to each other as they are driving west on Highway One.

I watch on, as top cover in the Vector, facing away to the north and our flank. My goggles are snug around my eyes, shemagh pulled up around my face, hiding me beneath a veil. The drive back to camp is a frenzy of dust and heat. The winds have shifted and are blowing from the east, at our heels, and spinning up dust from the desert to urge us on. The day is bright, hot, and the winds bring no relief, as dust and sand bite at my hands and the exposed skin on my face. No-one talks on our radio headsets whilst we drive back to camp, and I am lost in thought as I point my machine gun across the plains towards the mountains of the north. I have IRT tomorrow. I am hiding behind my gun, invisible, a stranger in a foreign land who wants nothing more than to see green chalk downs and feel the grass underneath his feet, instead of the endless grey of Helmand.

◊ ◊ ◊ ◊ ◊

We make our way back into camp after a time, and as the wagons are being prepared for another patrol, I try and find our unit Intelligence Officer to give my SigInt report to. He shrugs, an echo of Jamshed, when I find him and tell him I have a translation of some enemy signals to give him. I try and tell him about Talib Amidullah being a local leader, and the Farsi used whenever the other Taliban spoke to him.

'Radio chatter, nothing useful. Don't bother next time, it just makes work for you and me.'

54. ANOTHER DAY ON IRT

Another day comes, and with it another dash to the flight line, swapping sleep for the chill of the early day. With a flurry of boots, us infantrymen and the team of medics run off the concrete pan and up the loading ramp, and as we scramble into our seats the Chinook clamours into the sky. We soar high, and fast. Minutes pass, then we descend lower and lower. No-one shoots at us as the helicopter howls amongst fields and compounds at low altitude, and I rush out with the rest of the infantry team when the wheels bounce down. We have landed in Sangin, close to a platoon house. We take up ground on a ditch line and wait.

A stretcher comes, the old type, wood and canvas. I barely notice, hunkered down behind my gun, watching out at grasslines and treelines across the fields.

The call comes, a hoarse shout almost lost against the wild rotor wash, and I push myself to my feet and stagger into a low run back towards the Chinook.

Blast injuries. Bad ones. There is nothing else to say.

Morning mist is close around us, as the days and hours of this soldier's life have closed around him. He can see no further than minutes, and they will slip through his fingers

235

as a paramedic holds his hand. She gently brushes a drop of dried blood from his cheek with a latex-gloved thumb, and there is nothing left in the world for him but these last tiny gestures of kindness.

The Chinook roars, and the minutes fall away. He loses consciousness just north of FOB Juno.

We lift his corpse-heavy stretcher to dash to the ambulance, the pretence must continue until a doctor declares it is over. We load the stretcher, and the doors slam shut.

Half an hour later, the tannoy crackles. 'Op Minimise is now in effect. I say again, Op Minimise is now in effect. End of message. End of broadcast.' We are shrouded now in a pall of silence.

55. REAR SANGAR

Finally, I have made it to rear sangar. The days are winding on, spooling the sun around this country in a flaming arc of beauty, and no-one here sees or cares. If you could stop the clockwork soldiers in their tracks, and step out of your body, soaring into the heavens, you will see — what will you see? The cleanest, clearest skies. Dust, and mountains. And men in their shadow, teeming like ants, toiling to kill one another, barely looking up at the wonders around them.

How can I describe the feeling? Of watching out into the desert as the deepest, richest hints of the last darkness are slowly washed into a thousand imperial shades, and then by inches the dazzling cobalt skies creep through. Gun oil clings to my fingers, dust in the pores of my skin, and through weary eyes I see in a new day.

Graffiti scrawls cover the concrete sangar, thickest at head height, all around me. Some have inked their regimental badges on the back wall, where afternoon shafts of light will lance their way through the blast screen gaps. I see Parachute Regiment wings, Commando daggers. A motto: *Semper Fidelis*. A Danish flag, a hand grasping a bayonet. I see operational dates, Herrick 5 through Herrick

9. Badges, mottoes, dates, and names. Names upon names. I am encased in names; the air is heavy with them. Many carry a date next to them, some simply 'RIP', some both. My gaze settles on an inscription:

In a universe so vast and ageless, a man's worth can only be measured by the size of his sacrifice. To Guardsman Daryl Hickey.

The sun is blazing down now, striking the morning in furious yellow and white, and I stand alone in a fortress of concrete, sharing sentry with memories of the dead.

56. ADMIN DAY

The last days of Herrick 9 are upon us. New FOBs and platoon houses are being built around Nad Ali, and a large swathe of our patrol area has been taken over by other units. FOB Tombstone has been replaced with Camp Leatherneck, a huge new base for the US Marines to operate from, and they have taken our western wadi. FOB Argyll has subsumed our southern patrol routes into the new unit's Areas of Operations. Now on patrol, we stay close to Highway One or the central wadi. We don't even roam the northern edges anymore, the wild stony hills where the Russian minefields lie in silent wait, as FOB Juno have taken everything to the edge of Highway One. Confined to our reduced AO, we cross sewage river, zig-zagging and wheel-spinning our way past new poppy farmers' compounds. They are springing up closer and closer to camp, leeching off the foul and fertile run-off that the sewage plant spews out.

◊ ◊ ◊ ◊ ◊

The smaller, shorter patrols are also being half manned by the incoming unit who have come out to relieve us, which means that every man will get more hours of rest. So it is that one Thursday afternoon I find myself after a patrol, shaved and showered, in a clean shirt, and with nothing to do until O-Group that evening.

I have a thick woollen blanket that I can't pack in my backpack, so I have decided to give it to one of the interpreters as a present. Jamshed is at prayer when I go to find him in the interpreters' tent, so instead I find Jacobs, lounging outside the WMIK yard under the dappled semi-shade of a camouflage netting, topless, smoking a cigarette without a care in the world.

I join him, stripping off my shirt, letting the sunlight wash over me. I lean back on a wooden bench, sitting on the folded blanket like a cushion. We barely talk, instead sharing the silence, my cigarette burning idly between my fingers, and I scarcely bother to raise it to my lips. As we while away the time, we become the backdrop for an outgoing vehicle patrol who fill the armoured wagons just ahead of us with kit and ammunition. The top covers climb up and over the WMIK blast matting, driver and gunners swarm around. The patrol is a triad of khaki desert camouflage, olive green, gunmetal black. You could paint British Operations in Afghanistan with those three colours.

As the patrol is getting ready to move off, a whoosh comes from Bastion 2, and white vapour trails pour forth into a blue, blue sky. It is an outgoing fire mission, and the patrol whoops and cheers, stopping and turning to look, clapping each other on the shoulders excitedly.

Jacobs, too, is excited. 'Look at that Addy, that's the most beautiful thing I've ever seen!'

We sit under the camouflage netting until the vapour trails have long-since vanished and the sun has burnt the western sky a smouldering, deep red. With the evening nearing fast, the mosquitoes have started buzzing. Chill comes quickly, and I slip my shirt back on, and rise to attend O-Group.

On the way, I stop by Jamshed's tent. He greets me

with wide eyes and a happy smile when he sees his present and insists on giving me his email address so we will stay friends after I have left Afghanistan. He writes it on a crumpled piece of paper which he presses into my hand with both of his. 'Goodbye, Jamshed,' I say, and we shake hands.

Goodbye, Jamshed. Goodbye, Afghanistan. This was my last day outside the wire, I find out at O-Group that we are being moved to a transit camp next to the flight line.

57. WESTWARD BOUND

People think that home is a place. Those people are wrong. Home is both a time and a place, a perfect confluence of our feeling of belonging in the world, in a certain place that confirms and reinforces our feelings. When those two things come together — then and only then — we are home.

I will never get back the year of my life that I lost on my way to this day, my last day in Bastion. As I gaze into the perfect blue sky, and another fire mission streaks rocket-trails high into the morning light from Bastion 2 with a low whoosh, I know that my time has passed. Already the summer brings new changes — bulldozers toil day and night to construct the new American camp outside FOB Tombstone. This place that has been home these last months is changing to make me a stranger, both by time's relentless passing by, and by the physical reshaping of the familiar around us.

We are going home, they say, and I with them. We take

off at night from Bastion in a C-17, lights off, a company of men packed into the airframe. Engines strain, we shudder and climb, and after long minutes an announcement from the pilot,

'Departed Afghan airspace.'

To a man, we cheer. We pass through Oman, Cyprus, Brize Norton, Nottingham. We move from barracks to barracks, road moves and coaches follow in slow succession, and then — finally — we are at our barracks in Exeter.

◊ ◊ ◊ ◊ ◊

We are given liberty for the night, to parade the next day at 0800 sharp. Charlotte has come up from Plymouth and is staying at a local guest house. I find the address and book a taxi.

I am lost in thought as we rattle through the city. I am miles away, on Afghanistan's dusty plains. After longing for home for so long, part of me lingers back, left behind in the shadows of the mountains with Chris, and the dead — Afghan soldiers, American soldiers, British, and the little Afghan boy whose face I see when I close my eyes at night.

The taxi judders to a halt, and finally I am at my journey's end. I take a deep breath and step out of the car onto the evening-warmed cobbles of Exeter. The street is deserted, and sunlight weaves around an avenue of trees whilst behind me, the river's soft song rushes past. Birdsong from the riverbanks stirs memories of the past, of the boy climbing the hills for blackberries with his sister, of the boy running his hands through ears of grasses and sleeping in the summer sun. Afghanistan falls away from me, and in a surreal waking-dream I walk up the pathway, unsure what I will find in myself when my duty is over, and the dust is shaken from my boots. It is early evening, and my life is just beginning.

The door opens. 'Well — I'm back.' And that smile.

I am home.

END

ACKNOWLEDGMENTS

Heartfelt thanks are due to many, throughout the deployment to Helmand both in-country and at home; and since my return.

In Afghanistan: Thanks to the Lance Corporals and Corporals leading our patrols. To Chris, who led from the front and by example. To Aziz and Jamshed, who risked their lives by working for us. To the pilots of the IRT, into whose hands we trusted our lives every time we climbed up the ramp of the Chinook. To Kenny, who decided to give one more infrared flash before opening fire.

Back home: My thanks to the ladies of Exeter for keeping us supplied by air freight when the British Army ran low on rations. To Maggie for her whisky-smuggling skill. To the families of the Rifle Regiment, for whom the ordeal of a loved one's deployment was borne without the comradeship we could call on.

Since my return: Thanks to Brigadier Brian Parritt, for his kind words of encouragement and assistance in reviewing an early draft. To Oliver and Kate, for their review and suggestions. To James from the Bloody Eleventh, for his honest critique and endorsement.

Thanks to my parents, for their support before, during and after the deployment.

Thanks in no small measure to Charlotte, for seeing the best in me and sticking with me these many years.

GLOSSARY

AH: Attack Helicopter.

ATO: Ammunition Technician Officer. A bomb disposal expert.

AO: Area (of) Operations. The area we are given to patrol.

BFBS: British Forces Broadcasting Station.

Bastion: Camp Bastion. A large operating base in Helmand desert.

Cas: Casualty.

CQM: Company Quarter Master. Serjeant in charge of stores and equipment.

ECAS: Emergency Close Air Support.

EFI: Expeditionary Forces Institute. A small messroom for ranks to relax in.

EOD: Explosive Ordnance Disposal. The unit that an ATO is part of.

EWD: Electronic Warfare Devices.

FAC: Forward Air Controller.

FLET: Forward Line, Enemy Troops.

FLOT: Forward Line, Own Troops.

FOB: Forward Operating Base. Smaller base that houses a company.

GPMG: General Purpose Machine Gun.

GMLRS: Guided Multiple Launch Rocket System.

Hexiblock: Solid fuel burned in a stove to heat water or rations.

Highway One: The concrete road built by the Russians that links the farthest provinces of Afghanistan together.

HLS: Helicopter Landing Site.

IDF: Indirect Fire — mortars, rockets.

IED: Improvised Explosive Device.

IR: Infrared.

IRT: Incident Response Team.

ISAF: International Security Assistance Force.

LMG: Light Machine Gun. A compact, short-barrelled weapon.

LSW: Light Support Weapon. A long-barrelled variant of the standard British rifle, with an extended range.

M60: American machine gun.

Minimi: FN Minimi, an alternative name for the LMG.

NCO: Non-Commissioned Officer.

OC: Officer Commanding. In charge of a company.

OEF: Operation Enduring Freedom — name given to the US mission to Afghanistan.

PX: Post (e)Xchange.

R&R: Rest and Recuperation.

RPG: Rocket Propelled Grenade.

TIC: Troops in Contact.

WMIK: Weapons Mounted Installation Kit — an armoured Land Rover.

Zero: The Ops Room radio call sign.

ABOUT THE AUTHOR

Charles Addison "Addy" joined the Rifle Regiment in 2007 as a Reservist, and within weeks of completing basic training was called up for regular service with 1st Battalion Rifle Regiment. He deployed to Afghanistan with 3 Commando Brigade in 2008, serving as an infanteer on Operation Herrick 9. He left the army shortly after returning home, and married his girlfriend Charlotte. He now lives on the south coast of England with his family. This is his first publication.

PHOTO CREDITS

If you enjoyed this book, please consider leaving a review on Amazon. Thank you!

Printed in Great Britain
by Amazon